AF405432

Giftedness in Practice

Strengthening Personal Leadership in Gifted Adults

Rianne van de Ven

Dutch Editor: Deliana van der Meer, MEER! Woorden werken
Dutch final editing: Marjoleine Schlösser-Geuze, Met Goede Zin
English translation and editing: Sarah Carrington, Dr. Alice K. Burridge, Green Writing®
Photograph of author: Mirian Hendriks Photography
Design and layout: Kristel Guit, Studio Busser
Publisher: Donald Suidman, BigBusinessPublishers

ISBN: 9789493171435

Contents

Introduction

I discovered my giftedness in 2004, at the age of 33. My discovery led to an intensive personal process of integrating this newfound knowledge into my self-image. This process also inspired me to want to help other gifted people. After completing the postgraduate program "Coaching for Professionals," I started my coaching practice for gifted adults in 2007.

At first, I spent one day a week coaching alongside my regular job. After a few years, I decided to cut down my hours with my employer to spend two days a week working in my practice. I have been fully self-employed since 2016.

Besides coaching gifted people, I conduct research and give lectures and training courses. I have brought together my experience in this book. I feel the need to share my experience in counseling with others. I turned 50 this year and have entered a new phase in my life. Although I never want to stop learning and feel comfortable in the role of an eager student, I also experience a certain maturity in my profession. Training and supervising other professionals have become an increasingly important part of my work.

Therefore, my book is not aimed directly at gifted adults themselves, although they will surely benefit from reading it. This book is intended specifically for those who provide guidance to gifted people or encounter them in their practice or the workplace.

Because gifted people are a minority in the population, they are considered 'atypical.' Many gifted people feel somewhat disconnected from the people around them. Overcoming this requires an effort on the part of gifted people themselves as well as those around them. During my coaching, we explore both. So this book is also aimed at the people around gifted people.

Not all my statements in this book are supported by scientific research. A lot is also based on my experiences in practice and observations and the patterns I see in them. That is why I would like to stress that my client group is specific: it concerns gifted people who go to a coach to start working on specific questions.

The structure of this book reflects the coaching process that I go through with clients. Taking a bird's-eye view of this process, the main steps involved are recognizing, normalizing, processing, growing, using, and maintaining. The people in the client's environment also play a role. Not every step in the process is relevant to every client, and the order is not set in stone. Each client receives an individualized approach. The client investigates, learns, specifics, processes, renews, integrates, and utilizes.

Some clients stop or start halfway through. They all have different needs, which they explain to me so that I can coach them accordingly.

With this book, I hope to offer insights that will help people recognize and deal with their giftedness or that of a friend, partner, or colleague. In particular, I hope that my own experiences will be helpful to other professionals who occasionally or frequently offer guidance to gifted adults.

Rianne van de Ven, October 2021

Preface to the English translation

After publishing this book in Dutch in 2021, it is now available in English; this requires some context about giftedness in The Netherlands for the international reader.

Before 2000, no educational programs were available for gifted children in The Netherlands. Even today, no certainty exists that gifted children will be identified as such at an early age or provided with the specialized educational support they require. However, there is a growing interest in gifted children in the Netherlands, and because of this new attention, many adults are beginning to recognize their own giftedness.
The gifted adults in my practice have a strong developmental potential that often has not been identified in their childhood. When they discover their giftedness late(r) in life, they often require help adjusting and integrating this in their self-image.
Even in countries where gifted education programs have existed for a long time, not every gifted child is identified. Consequently, in these countries, my experience in working with adult giftedness identification can also be of great use to professionals who guide, coach, counsel, or treat gifted adults.

Rianne van de Ven, May 2022

Reader's guide

The stories I use during coaching sessions in my practice form the foundation of this book. This does not mean that every chapter or every section applies to every gifted individual. Each client follows their specific path within the coaching process. For this book, I put all the relevant aspects of the coaching process in a logical order.

Chapter 1 is about how I see giftedness. My clients are people who already know or strongly suspect that they are gifted but have not known this for long, with all of the consequences this entails. What does giftedness look like for them? What do you do as a mental health professional if you think one of your clients may be gifted? What does giftedness look like for these clients? Do they still have doubts? How do CoreTalents work? I close this chapter with the Delphi Model of Giftedness, with which I enjoy working.
In Chapter 2, I provide general and in-depth information about giftedness. What issues do gifted people encounter? How do they differ from non-gifted people? How does giftedness explain a person's behavior, and how does the outside world react to this? How do gifted people create? What about gender identity?
Chapter 3 deals with how my clients process their recently discovered giftedness. Of course, this is different for each client because it depends on how their development up to that point has affected their lives.
Chapter 4 describes how clients learn to deal with their giftedness and its implications. They develop a new self-image.
Learning new skills is of great importance to better cope with the less positive aspects of giftedness. What are executive functions? Why are these skills often less developed in gifted people? In this chapter, I also discuss how gifted people can improve their communication skills. In addition, I address effective influencing and self-care skills.

Chapter 5 is about using one's potential. In this phase of the process, the client and I look at their passions, of which gifted people often have more than one. How can you convert your passions into a job? What does the job application process look like? I also deal with the process of finding meaning, an important part of a gifted person's life. In Chapter 6, I describe the role of the gifted person's environment and how it can support their process.

The final chapter discusses the conclusion of the coaching process. The client and I look at whether and how they can continue without my help. What do they need? What tools can they use or are good to work with? At the end of this chapter, I write about going "beyond the label," meaning that discovering their giftedness initially plays a major role in a client's life. There is often a great sense of relief, and this new insight has to be discovered and experienced. During this often-temporary period, the client is preoccupied with the theme of 'giftedness.' To me, "beyond the label" means that someone has integrated their giftedness into their self-image and views it as one among many aspects of their identity.

1

Recognizing

1.1. About giftedness

The concept of 'giftedness' is still in its infancy. There are many definitions of giftedness, but none are universally accepted. Most definitions and models come from the world of education and are based on studies of children. While attention to giftedness in education is important, there is more to giftedness than that. Someone doesn't stop being gifted when they finish school or turn 18. A gifted person remains gifted throughout their life, and giftedness affects more than just education. Giftedness also explains differences between people in the areas of physical and mental health and work.

Attention to giftedness in adults is an even more recent development in scientific research. Therefore, research on this topic is still scarce. The Dutch Gifted Adults Foundation (*Instituut Hoogbegaafdheid Volwassenen*, IHBV) dedicates itself to this theme. The Netherlands leads the way in this respect internationally. Fortunately, the scope of giftedness is also expanding in other countries.

In the Netherlands, a clear outline has been formulated that appeals to me greatly. It reads:

"A gifted person is a quick and clever thinker, able to deal with complex matters. Autonomous, curious and passionate. A sensitive and emotionally rich individual, with great imagery, living intensely. He or she enjoys being creative." [1]

---

1 Kooijman-van Thiel, 2008

The Delphi Model of Giftedness that accompanies this outline
visualizes giftedness as follows:

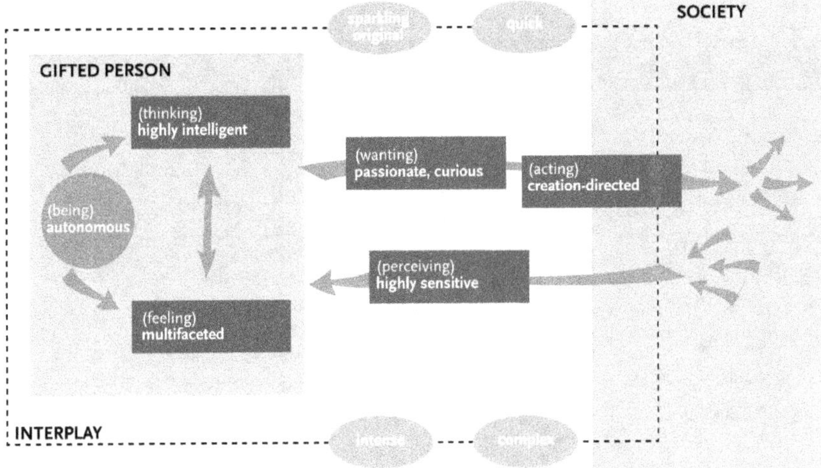

From: M.B.G.M. Kooijman - van Thiel (ed.). *Highly Gifted. Obvious? On Identity and Image of Gifted Persons.* OYA Productions, 2008

According to the Delphi Model of Giftedness, the characteristics of giftedness are:

The inner world of the gifted individual:

Being	Thinking	Feeling
Autonomous	Highly intelligent	Multifaceted
• Makes their own judgments • Makes their own decisions • Sticks with their decisions until something better comes along	• Highly analytical by nature • Matrix thinking: multiple simultaneous tracks, levels, and moments • Metacognition: thinking about the matrix itself • Pattern recognition • Easily alternating between divergent and convergent thinking • Strong associative power • Good working memory and long-term memory	• Many simultaneous emotions • Sometimes so many emotions that they need to withdraw • Strongly interlaced • Nuanced and colorful

The gifted individual in relation to society:

Wanting	Acting	Perceiving
Passionate and curious	Creation-directed	Highly sensitive
• Wanting a lot • Preferably right away • Always looking for something new • Inquisitive, wanting to discover • Clinging on • Persistent • Gets into a flow easily	• Always busy making something and enjoying doing so: a model, process, theory, plan, technique, method, analysis, overview, invention, improvement, game, idea, product, puzzle, painting, or piece of music • Worlds of thought, structures, stories, images	• There are indications of a gradually different neurological system: more, thinner, and faster nerves, more sensitive sensory neurons, more and faster synapses, a brain active in more places at the same time. • Everything arrives at once, fully nuanced, with great precision, and with its full weight

Intense, complex, quick, and creative are the characteristic features of the interaction between a gifted person and their environment. I also refer to these as the dimensions of which a gifted person must be extra aware because these are the areas in which they can become disconnected from their environment.

1.2. How I see giftedness

I often say: "Line up three hundred gifted people, and you'll have three hundred different individuals. What binds them together is best described in the Delphi Model."
I see giftedness as a combination of different elements. It is not just about high intelligence but about the overall picture. Their high intelligence enables quick and complex thinking but also intense feeling. Gifted people understand many nuances that escape those who are not gifted. Gifted people grasp situations more quickly and seek to understand them. Gifted people are creative, often have several passions, and therefore do not fit into the ready-made categories that people define for each other. Because of these differences, gifted people are at risk of feeling disconnected from their environment.

Who are my clients?

Giftedness is receiving more attention now than ever before. Most research has focused on giftedness among children, and multiple books have been written about it. Some schools also have programs that cater to the needs of these children. There is no doubt that progress is being made. More and more adults were identified as being gifted as children. However, most of my clients did not find out they were gifted until they were adults and did not have access to any special programs at school. When people find out that they are gifted later in life, this usually means they are experiencing specific problems or issues. People don't go looking for answers when life is going smoothly. Therefore, the insights into giftedness, which my clients gain while coached by me, often lead to a grieving process. Many clients experience a strong sense of loss for things they never had. How different could their lives have been? Some go through this process alone, while others seek help.

Clients who turn to me for coaching have varying views of their own intelligence and intelligence in general. There are those who:
• think that being gifted is a requirement for my coaching. They then mean an IQ score that qualifies for Mensa membership (a

score in the 98th or 99th percentile; for most tests, this is a score of 130 or higher). They take an IQ test before coming to me;
- have not yet taken a test and ask me if that is a problem;
- identify with the characteristics of giftedness but do not have a corresponding IQ score;
- see an intelligence test as part of the process. For them, I include an IQ test supervised by a licensed psychologist.

As a coach, my focus is on gifted people. My clients often ask me if I think they are gifted. I do not give definitive answers on this, although I see it in their behavior, such as their speed of understanding, their high level of abstraction, and their humor. Recognition based on these characteristics often brings great relief. Suddenly giftedness seems to explain everything, and some clients attribute everything to it. Everything revolves around giftedness, even their personality. That's fine at first. It's a mechanism that helps them move forward, but being gifted is only part of their identity. Because this part of their identity has long been overlooked, devoting lots of attention to it can have a healing effect. In my coaching, I use this temporary extra emphasis on the theme of 'giftedness' to help my clients improve their self-knowledge. This focus often fades into the background as the coaching process progresses. A personality is more than just intelligence.

To further clarify giftedness, I often use opposites and extremes and black and white thinking in my practice. Of course, the reality is much more nuanced, but the extreme dichotomy clarifies things immediately. Examples are gifted and not gifted, fixed and growth mindset, and top-down and bottom-up thinking.

My clients are highly diverse. They vary in gender, age, background, nationality, social position, and more. They are referred to me by the Dutch Unemployment Agency (UWV) as part of their reintegration program, private individuals, self-employed individuals, or offered a coaching program by their employer. They only have one thing in common: they display characteristics of giftedness.

The coaching needs of my clients

My clients' coaching needs are also very diverse. The following coaching goals are common:

- investigating whether the client is gifted
- increasing their self-knowledge
- learning to make the most of their potential
- reducing problems associated with fear of failure, fixed mindset, and procrastination
- improving competencies, such as communication skills or executive functions
- better self-care, especially for highly sensitive clients
- reintegration into work after illness, often after burnout or boreout
- career coaching, outplacement
- finding meaning

1.3. Gifted but unaware

Gifted people who do not know that they are gifted, who are unaware of their giftedness, often seek support from a mental health professional because they experience issues like fear of failure, procrastination, or avoidance. But following a diagnosis, therapy usually does not solve the problem because nothing is done about the underlying cause: the mismatch with their environment due to being gifted.

Everything falls into place when a client realizes they are gifted and understands what this means. The knowledge and implications of being gifted make them stronger and more self-aware. Understanding how their brain works, how they differ from non-gifted people, and what they can do about this gives them tools for action. It gives them space so that the initial symptoms decrease or even disappear altogether.

Some gifted people do not experience any difficulties related to their giftedness and have never wondered whether they are gifted. This group is also unaware. These people are often very successful and do not look for explanations for their situation. Or at least, not yet. They may well turn to a mental health professional later in life.

I also often observe that clients who have recently discovered their giftedness suddenly see gifted people all around them. Inspired by their newfound knowledge and enthusiasm about what this discovery brings them, they want to share this knowledge with other gifted people. Their new insights color their perception, and they see gifted people everywhere. It's like buying a new car. The first few weeks after buying it, you'll see cars of the same make or color everywhere.
This principle is also known as the Baader-Meinhof phenomenon or frequency illusion.

1.4. What giftedness looks like for my clients

"Am I gifted or not?" That is often the first question my clients ask. This question implies that there is a threshold to determine this. But such a threshold does not exist. There is no such thing as a giftedness test either. Linguistically it would be better to say that somebody exhibits strong characteristics of giftedness. After all, according to the Delphi Model, giftedness has multiple characteristics.
An intelligence test is not a giftedness test. An IQ test indicates the IQ level, but does not hold information about the other characteristics. I do not require an IQ test before taking on a client. If someone doesn't score in the 98th or 99th percentile, I don't necessarily assume they are not gifted. The timing of the test can influence the score. How stressed was the person when they took it? Were they able to concentrate? Were they affected by an underlying trauma during the test? Taking the test is an achievement, and many gifted people haven't learned how to give it their best.
However, the other side is clear: a score in the 98th or 99th percentile reinforces the presumption of giftedness. I don't believe that anyone can fake intelligence.

Some of my clients are unsure about whether to get themselves tested. I understand their doubts. The test can be very stressful, which can affect the result. Clients who first decide not to take an IQ test sometimes change their minds once they have gained more self-confidence. I also have many clients who don't feel the need to have their intelligence evaluated. Their high intelligence is reflected in their social achievements, such as a successful academic career, including obtaining a Ph.D.

To me, an IQ test is not essential. During the intake interview, I assess whether a client could benefit from looking at themselves from the perspective of the catch-all term 'giftedness.' During the intake, I often see giftedness "in action" by switching gears quickly, digressing, and making connections at multiple levels. I evaluate clients during the intake, and if I observe these characteristics, I am prepared to start the coaching process under the assumption that my client is gifted.

1.5. CoreTalents

Many of my clients have previously experienced some form of assessment or a color test. Often, they don't fully identify with the resulting report. I experienced this myself during my career. When I was introduced to the CoreTalents Analysis in 2013, a new world opened up for me. The CoreTalents Analysis is an assessment tool developed in Belgium by Danielle Krekels. The tool is ideally suited to gifted people. They identify with and feel completely understood in the report. While reading my CoreTalents report, I felt completely understood for the first time. This moved me because previous assessments had often left me feeling shortchanged. The method is based on more than 12,000 interviews and establishes a relationship between someone's play behavior as a child and a CoreTalent of the adult they have become. The method was scientifically validated in 2015 as being highly reliable. For experts: it has a reliability of .84 Cronbach's alpha, comparable to the Big Five personality test reliability. The CoreTalents Analysis measures 23 different CoreTalents. A CoreTalent has three components: nature, potential, and intrinsic motivation. There are more than 94 billion possible CoreTalents constellations. Instead of being pigeonholed, the client receives a specific, nuanced, and individual profile.

The analysis works as follows. Roughly speaking, scores for CoreTalents are expressed as small, partial, or strong. A small CoreTalent does not offer joy and requires energy. A strong CoreTalent does provide joy and plenty of energy. Partial means that a CoreTalent does not guide a person's life or career choices. The partial CoreTalents are weighted depending on the other CoreTalents within the full constellation of 23. If clients have many strong CoreTalents, I advise them to focus on them and leave the partial talents for what they are. After all, addressing all their strong CoreTalents is a big enough challenge. If someone has many small CoreTalents, I explain that spending time on their partial talents can be positive, but also here, spending time on their strong CoreTalents provides the most energy. Clients should pay minimal attention to their small CoreTalents.

This method was not solely developed for gifted people, and it works for anyone. However, we see that this method captures the complexity and multitude of talents of gifted individuals very well. This is probably because Danielle Krekels exhibits many characteristics of giftedness herself. Moreover, she ran a recruitment agency for highly skilled and technical personnel while conducting the interviews. She conducted many of the 12,000 interviews with people from her recruitment agency's database. More than two percent of this population were likely gifted. Therefore, gifted individuals were probably overrepresented in her population, making this analysis suitable for gifted people.

The CoreTalents Analysis distinguishes desire (intrinsic motivation) from ability. Many gifted people can do things well or above average, including things they don't really enjoy.
It is, therefore, possible that a gifted person does something they are good at or are asked to do without it giving them energy. While the compliments the gifted person receives or the results they achieve may give them some satisfaction, this is not the same as the energy they get from using their strong CoreTalents.

I use the CoreTalents Analysis for every client. I explain that their problem probably isn't their ability but their energy management. What gives them energy, and what takes it away? This is an important and decisive factor in a client's sustainable employability and well-being. Frequently using a small talent drains someone's energy, which increases the risk of burnout. Insufficient use of a strong talent also takes a lot of energy and can lead to boreout.

You can achieve sustainable employability and feel good about yourself by frequently using strong talents and rarely or not using small talents.

When clients recognize and identify with their talents after a CoreTalents Analysis, this often releases energy and inspiration to start working on their careers. Contraindications for a CoreTalents Analysis are a personality disorder or acquired brain injury. In these cases, the development from childhood to adulthood has been severely disrupted, and the method cannot be used. Childhood trauma can also provide distorted results because it may mean that a client started doing things for reasons other than enjoying them. However, potential talents remain the same, even if a traumatized child develops differently. What the child enjoyed or dreamed of doing remains valid. The analysis reveals these talents as strong CoreTalents even in cases of childhood trauma. The things the child did not do are more difficult to assess. These become small CoreTalents, while the reasons for not doing these things may have been external factors, such as being punished or fear of punishment. In that case, the profile is incomplete, and there is only certainty about the energy sources. This information is still highly relevant for career issues. Therefore, it is essential that a senior analyst performs the analysis in cases where people suffer from childhood trauma.

Many people think that the toys a child is offered shape their play behavior. Danielle Krekels discovered that the opposite is true: children play with toys that appeal to them. Even in cases where children have only a few or no toys, they show their true nature in play behavior. For example, when they pick up a twig from a tree.

One child might use it to draw in the sand, while another might use a knife to carve it into a spear for role-playing. And yet another child might bend and shape the twig into a car and pretend to drive it around. Children actively look for what interests them. Avid readers who grow up in a home with few books, like me, are drawn to friends who have well-stocked bookshelves.

The CoreTalents Analysis validates the complexity and multifaceted talents of the gifted individual. The analysis confirms the gifted person's qualities. And that works. Every gifted person is different!
The CoreTalents Analysis is not a tool used to determine *whether* someone is gifted, but it does indicate *how* someone is gifted. When one client discovered her 21 (!) strong CoreTalents, I told her: "*She is all that.*" That brought her recognition and emotion. It is important for people to feel validated. Many clients have felt different all their lives and can clearly explain how and why after a CoreTalents Analysis. I often hear clients say afterward: "The report didn't tell me anything I didn't know already, but it's so nice to have it in writing." Knowledge about personal energy drains is also often meaningful to clients. Being good at something doesn't necessarily indicate that it energizes you.

Personal profile based on the Delphi Model

To help interpret their giftedness in life, I let my clients put together a personal profile based on the Delphi Model. This profile is a biographical assignment in which their life is viewed through the lens of giftedness. It highlights specific memories and events more than others. Clients use the characteristics of the Delphi Model to chart the course of their lives. This assignment focuses not only on negative experiences associated with their giftedness – which clients can name all too easily – but also on the positive side. What has giftedness brought them in life? For many clients, this may bring up memories of adventures they experienced by themselves or feelings of pride about how they solved a particular problem. These positive memories visibly give the client extra energy and space.

Normalizing

One of the first parts of coaching gifted people is to increase their knowledge about giftedness. How does giftedness work, and what are its consequences? Everyone takes themselves as a reference or starting point, but because a gifted person deviates from the average and is not representative, this comparison with others often results in major differences. A gifted person's inner world is more creative, faster, more intense, and more complex than that of a non-gifted person. This can clash, especially if someone doesn't understand the reason for these differences. Therefore, knowledge about one's giftedness is needed to put the perceived differences into perspective. Knowing what many gifted people have to deal with is a great boost to self-acceptance.

The gifted client learns to recognize the different aspects of their giftedness. The knowledge shared in this chapter initially provides insight into a specific aspect, followed by acceptance and solace.

2.1. Thinking further ahead (and back)

Gifted people think at a highly intelligent level, have a vast amount of knowledge at their disposal, and have a large working memory, so they have lots of knowledge and memories. Among other things, this enables them to plan further ahead.
It could be said that gifted people think twelve steps ahead, while non-gifted people think three steps ahead. These numbers are illustrative, not scientific.
Gifted people can grasp more steps and more consequences. This means that a gifted person needs more time to figure things out and form opinions. A gifted person first needs to get things straight in their mind.

We also see the difference in intelligence when looking back. A gifted person's working memory is larger than average and goes back further. As such, a gifted person has a lot of knowledge and memories at their disposal. I provide an example from my practice to illustrate this.

During a meeting, a client's colleague gives a speech that contradicts what they said in a previous meeting. My client realizes this immediately because they can clearly remember what the colleague said in a meeting four weeks ago. They can also picture it. They can visualize the green sweater the speaker was wearing, in which meeting room the particular meeting took place, and even the paintings on the wall. They hear the contradictory words. Depending on their personal experience, a gifted person may assume that this is deliberate deception. This usually isn't the case because the non-gifted person is completely unaware of what they said four weeks ago, at least at that moment. Many gifted people have an urge to point out such inconsistencies. But, unfortunately, they don't always do so diplomatically. The non-gifted person is then confronted with a contradiction in their statements of which they probably weren't aware. Not everyone responds positively to this.

Discussions between a gifted person and a non-gifted person often concern subjects realized by the gifted person but not (yet) by the non-gifted person.

A gifted person's working memory includes more steady knowledge, and they also have more in mind for the future. The final goal often lies further on the horizon. A gifted person is aware of more things and sees the bigger picture.

The following diagram represents this:

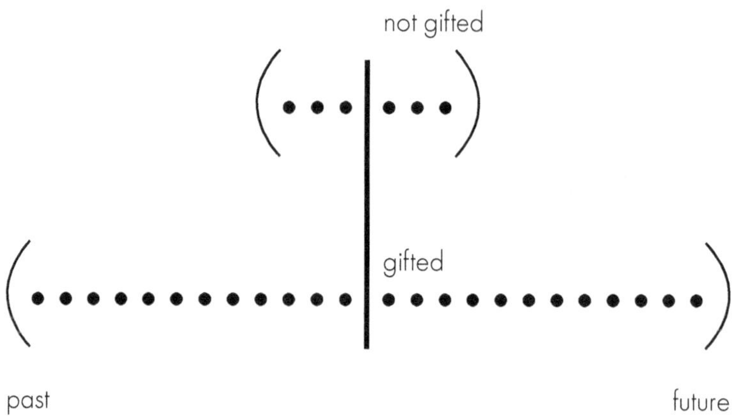

This diagram also shows why gifted people are so good at identifying patterns or their absence. They see more "dots."
A gifted person sees things that others don't yet see, meaning that what is obvious to a gifted person isn't necessarily obvious to someone else. Everyone views themselves as the default or norm and cannot imagine that another person sees something else. "Everyone sees what I see, don't they?" This assumption works for much of the population – non-gifted people.
However, it doesn't work for gifted people, which often results in a lack of understanding and can even lead to conflicts. My clients often tell me that they become suspicious in these situations or feel that they have been fooled.
Or they get frustrated because the other person doesn't see "it."
"How can they not see it? It's obvious, isn't it?" Particularly when people aren't yet aware of their giftedness, we see that they project their standards onto others. And others are often unable to live up to those standards.

A gifted person who is aware of this will ask the other (non-gifted) person how they see the situation so that the gifted person can tie in with this and possibly broaden the other person's horizon. My clients often tell me that they hate it when others attribute something to new insights. Couldn't those other people have realized this earlier, as they did? But when gifted people acknowledge that other people need more time to reach the same level of understanding, they can appreciate advancing insight and even steer toward it. By trying to tie in with how other people see things, gifted people can bridge the difference in perception and the time it takes to process information (learning).

When a gifted person receives and understands new information, they can give it a place in their mind. Therefore, they don't need to hear the same information twice. However, non-gifted people often need the power of repetition.

2.2. Speed and complexity

The way gifted people think is also faster and more complex. Because of this, a gifted person sees much more and is aware of things that others don't see. Not everyone sees what a gifted person sees. At least, not right away and not as quickly. This is also where things can go wrong in attunement with others.

Gifted people are often also highly sensitive. More on this can be found later in this chapter. Being highly sensitive lets gifted people perceive more nuances and thus have more information at their disposal. Because they perceive abstract patterns more easily, gifted people are quicker to see how things work. And once they know how something works, they understand the art of generalization and can apply it to other situations. As a result, gifted people can make leaps that are difficult or even impossible for non-gifted people to follow.

2.3. Top-down learning

Gifted people prefer a top-down approach to learning. This approach means that they like to figure out and understand things for themselves. They want to understand how something works and then generalize this understanding to similar situations. Practicing doesn't always work for them. In fact, they often hate it. Unfortunately for gifted people, the (Dutch) education system mostly offers bottom-up learning.
This means that something is explained and demonstrated, after which students practice it. It doesn't require understanding how things work, just recognition based on repetition.
When gifted people see how something works, they start working on it. Until then, they often think about exactly what's involved. This process can take a long time, making non-gifted people impatient. They just want to get started, which can cause friction. A gifted person wants to know exactly how things work and what to expect. Which tangents are there to explore? What if something goes wrong? Gifted people desire certainty, and uncertainty can paralyze them.

This certainty does not exist for non-gifted people, so they learn to handle uncertainty much earlier in life. They are used to not being able to fully grasp many situations. Gifted people benefit from having this certainty as children and young adults. Still, as they age and the context becomes more complicated than before, gifted people should also learn to deal with uncertainty. Gifted people, therefore, often start developing strategies for this later.

The following table shows the most significant differences between bottom-up and top-down learning.

Bottom-up	Top-down
Demonstrate – explain – practice	Find out for yourself – understand
Repeat until you recognize it	Less practice; it's about understanding
Learn by seeing the similarities	Learn by seeing the differences
Act upon recognition, automate, predict	Able to apply the system and the rules to any situation
Take action based on probability	Take action based on certainty
Inductive reasoning	Deductive reasoning
Experience-based learning	Goal or meaning-based learning

The top-down learning strategy gives gifted people great certainty, which they need to get started. Gifted people are not used to uncertainty. Even with an exceptionally high degree of certainty, gifted people can feel paralyzed and really need that last bit of certainty.

Non-gifted people are often bottom-up thinkers who need a reasonable probability to get started.

When gifted people are given a task they can grasp entirely based on their intelligence, they complete this task without any problems. Gifted people can follow the top-down method with a 100 percent success rate to carry out such a task. However, most tasks are not within their range of vision in adult life, and there is no 100 percent certainty. Gifted people will try to achieve the highest possible degree of certainty for tasks like these. They spend a long time preparing, weighing up the pros and cons, and considering possible outcomes and scenarios. They will not get started until they have enough certainty. Sometimes a gifted person may get stuck and cannot start at all. This can also be interpreted as procrastination or fear of failure.

This pursuit of certainty seems inconsistent with another side of giftedness. Gifted people can be very enterprising and adventurous. Experimentation and being open to new experiences also characterize giftedness. It is not about achievement and certainty in relation to preventing mistakes but about gaining new experiences.

Preferred style

Gifted people prefer a top-down thinking and learning style, but this does not mean being unable to learn from the bottom up. For example, getting a driver's license is bottom-up learning, and it involves a lot of practice in a car. The more miles someone drives, the better they become at driving. Experience-based learning usually isn't an enjoyable method for a gifted person. They would prefer to learn to drive by reading a book about a car, studying the car and its driver, and then using what they've learned to simply get in the car and drive off perfectly. Unfortunately, that's not how it works. There is more to it. For driving, as for many other situations in adult life, 100 percent certainty is an illusion. Situations and problems become more complicated as people age, making it even more difficult for gifted adults to achieve the degree of certainty they need. In that case, the top-down method is not the best strategy for handling a situation. Gifted people must therefore learn to deal with uncertainty. Many of the gifted people I see in my practice are not yet able to do this. They have not developed alternative strategies for when they don't see "it."

Reasoning based on rules

One aspect of top-down learning involves searching for general rules that can be applied repeatedly. A gifted person understands how it works, which provides certainty. To discover a rule, gifted people ask questions about why. Gifted children also do this frequently. When adults do this at work, it can cause problems. Team members and managers don't always understand why a gifted person asks those questions and may become irritated.

They sometimes interpret asking "why" as calling something into question or holding someone accountable. People may even feel intimidated. I write more about this in Chapter 3.

Bottom-up learning is about creating a situation in which something has a reasonable chance of success. A bottom-up learner lives and works with uncertainty every day without being paralyzed by it. They know that the problem does not have to be solved on the first attempt and that making mistakes is part of the game.
The desire for certainty associated with the top-down style explains why gifted people often suffer from fear of failure, procrastination, avoidance, and, in more severe cases, certain anxiety disorders. The gifted people I see in my practice have difficulty dealing with uncertainty.

Pitfalls of top-down thinking, learning, and creating
- Not learning to deal with uncertainty, surprises, or setbacks
- Not learning how to learn: setting goals, following a plan, evaluating (self-directed learning)
- Fear of failure
- Perfectionism
- Procrastination, or wanting to "see" everything before you can get started
- Not realizing that it works differently for others

I always tell gifted clients not to unlearn top-down thinking! The top-down way of thinking is very powerful and has many advantages. But it is not always the smartest approach and sometimes comes with disadvantages. Gifted people should thus develop alternative strategies to expand their repertoire of skills. With multiple strategies, they can deal appropriately with situations that are not entirely predictable and in which 100 percent certainty is not possible.

What do top-down thinkers look for? And what behavior is associated with this? The following summary is inspired by the Dutch article *Top-down denken* (*Top-down thinking*) by Jet Barendrecht. I have rewritten it in the context of adults in relation to work.

Top-down thinking among gifted people

Top-down thinking is:
- thinking from the top down
- from the whole to its parts
- from a goal to the action
- from a framework to its elements
- from the total to its components
- from overview to details
- from the why to the how
- from an annual to a weekly to a daily schedule

Top-down thinkers are looking for:
- the overview
- the whole
- the goal
- the framework
- the total
- the why

How top-down thinkers behave:
- They ask many questions about how and why.
- They try to catch all implications in a single answer to a question (and sometimes have to think for a while before answering).
- They ask general questions when they want to know something specific.
- They need time to switch from one "system" to another.
- They start the story halfway through. The first part has already taken place in their mind. They forget that they only verbalize part of their thought process and often skip what is obvious to them.

- They ask for an explanation if it fits into the system and ignore the structure of someone else's story (for example, in presentations).

2.4. Addicted to certainty

It is normal for gifted people to think and feel a lot. They can look at situations from multiple perspectives and at various levels of abstraction. Each perspective is associated with different emotions. I often say: "A gifted person never has just one thought about something, and the same is often true about feelings." This multiplicity and complexity of thoughts and feelings require good self-management. Or, from the perspective of the Delphi Model: taking charge of *highly intelligent thinking* and *multifaceted feeling* based on the *autonomous being*.

Many of today's gifted adults in the Netherlands did not receive an appropriate education as children, resulting in not fully developing certain necessary skills. Consequently, they often find that they never learned how to learn.
This not only applies to study skills but also to behavior and attitudes toward work or making choices. They have not developed enough strategies to deal with situations.
When gifted people grasp a situation at once and then do what is necessary, they will feel little satisfaction. They do not perceive this as a success and will have difficulty accepting compliments.
When gifted people do something successfully on their first attempt, there is little room or need for self-reflection. Evaluation is not necessary because it went well right away.
But if a gifted person does not fully grasp the situation at once, they may develop feelings of anxiety and panic. An overall picture of the complete path to be traveled (meaning 100 percent certainty) is needed to get started. If that doesn't work, but they get started anyway, everything a gifted person does is so well thought out that there is a chance of reality becoming second to

the perfect picture in their mind. This guarantees disappointments, opposition, and setbacks, things gifted people don't tolerate well. When they fail to carry out something successfully, gifted people soon blame themselves. I see this low tolerance for uncertainty in my practice on a daily basis. I work with my clients on expanding their repertoire of skills to deal with uncertainty and be more likely to act based on probability.

Uncertainty and intolerance of mistakes also cause many of my clients to worry, an exaggerated form of preparation in which they run through every possible scenario. Reality may not deviate from this. When reality differs from what my clients expected, I see that many of them are quick to blame themselves. A common thought is, "I should have seen that beforehand." When a gifted person does not grasp the whole situation at once, the goal is beyond their horizon. It then helps to set sub-goals and think about what is possible. Or, "when will the probability be high enough to get started?"

The following diagram shows this:

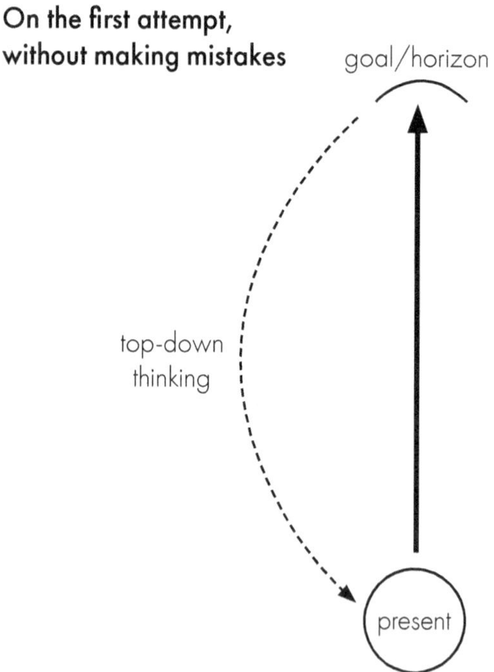

Alternative:

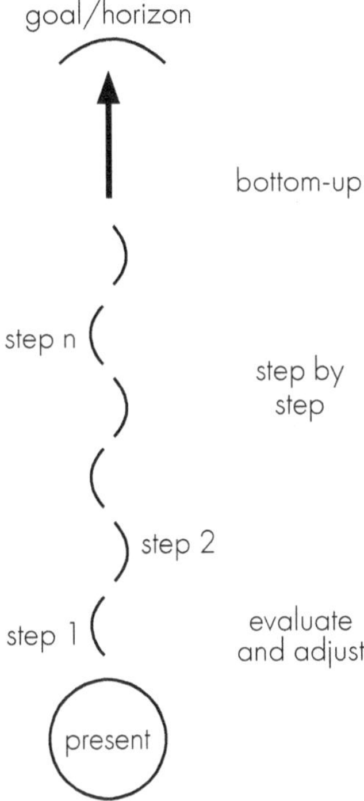

After seeing the "on the first attempt, without making mistakes" diagram, my clients realize that they have to start verbalizing their uncertainty. And instead of a final goal, I teach my clients to set sub-goals and focus more on the process than the final result. They can use these sub-goals to factor in the necessary certainty and get started. Of course, things can still turn out differently than one of the ten scenarios a gifted person has worked out in their mind. Reality is and will continue to be unpredictable, but it is still the reality. Many of my clients find it difficult to accept things for what they are, despite having many valuable talents that enable them to respond to this reality in the here and now. They have astute powers of perception and creativity to allude to reality on the spot.

Although the theories of self-directed learning come from the field of education, some of their principles are also useful for my clients. I divide these principles into three phases: before – during – after. It is about preparation (before), execution according to plan (during), and evaluation (after). A certain amount of awareness is often enough to bring about improvement.

Preparation (before)	Execution (during)	Evaluation (after)
Keywords: • Preparation • Several steps ahead • Anticipation • Working out scenarios • Assessing risks	*Keywords:* • Using creativity • Powers of perception • Execution according to plan • Adjusting where necessary	*Keywords:* • Evaluation • (Deeper) information processing (a characteristic of high sensitivity)
Positive if: • Greater sense of certainty • Getting started with sufficient probability • Defining research or learning objectives	*Positive if:* • Accepting reality • Assessing and adjusting in the here and now	*Positive if:* • New intentions • Actions to correct as needed • Learning from experience
Negative if: • Increase in panic • Increase in uncertainty	*Negative if:* • Condemning reality • Getting hung up on ideal	*Negative if:* • Blaming (oneself), it should have been done differently

During coaching, my client and I evaluate events in their lives and use them as a basis to set new goals and see when the client can try something new. We then reflect on this in the next coaching session. Based on the knowledge gained in the evaluation, we formulate new goals. The process then starts all over again. This is experience-based learning. The idea is that the client will learn to do this independently in the future, without my guidance.

Preparation

I see many gifted adults who either do not prepare (and just do something) or spend far too long preparing without getting started until they have created the necessary certainty. These issues occur in all kinds of situations at work and in their private lives. Examples are important decisions, conversations, meetings, projects, assignments, or writing texts. Panic, fear of failure, and procrastination often play a role in having to achieve. Good preparation requires two things from a gifted person: a sense of "sufficient probability" to get started and a plan with learning or research objectives. Such a plan does not necessarily have to be in writing. Making the plan is about the inner dialogue, the conversation with oneself about how to approach something that does not provide 100 percent certainty. There are things a person cannot know beforehand and does not encounter until the execution phase. Gifted people can benefit from defining goals or sub-goals for what they are unsure about. They can ask themselves questions like: "What do I want to learn? What can I do differently? When can I do it differently?" Confidence and self-reliance are important, knowing what strengths they can rely on during the execution phase.

Preparation is ineffective when it leads to feelings of panic and increased uncertainty. Clients who often experience this worry a lot and have trouble sleeping. I try to help my clients turn their worrying into "healthy preparation." The ability of gifted people to work out many scenarios can cause them to keep thinking. Especially when a subject is close to the gifted person's heart, it makes sense that they want to use their cognitive ability to make things go well. But all of that thinking inevitably ends with a decision, a choice, or an intention. It serves a purpose. It helps to plan this thinking, enabling a gifted person to take control, which prevents thinking from turning into worrying. When steps are repeated while thinking, there are no new arguments, and the preparation phase is finished. A good question for a gifted person to ask in that case is: "Am I ready to make the decision or start the execution phase?"

Execution

In the execution phase, my clients and I work on "executing according to plan." Gifted people possess many strong qualities they can use during this phase, such as keen powers of perception, creativity, and the ability to switch gears quickly when things do not go as they hoped or expected. The execution phase is positive if the person accepts reality despite setbacks or surprises because they can be adjusted at any moment. My clients often condemn reality when it deviates from the ideal picture in their minds. They remain stuck in that ideal and say things like: "It shouldn't be this way." They certainly shouldn't ignore these feelings and should acknowledge them instead, but it is essential that they remain constructive and do not become victims. I try to get them to follow through and ask themselves questions like: "What *can* I do now?" The aims are to learn to think in terms of possibilities, appeal to their creativity, and look for options of getting help. Many of my clients are not good at this. They want to do it themselves because of their strong sense of autonomy. They don't want to be a burden to others, or they think they should be able to do it themselves.

What can help in this self-management phase is "The circle of 8." Many of my clients have this circle on display at home or work as a constant reminder. Unfortunately, I cannot find the source in the literature, and a good scientific foundation seems to be lacking, but it works well as a coaching tool.[2]

---

2 Van Doorn and Lingsma

The circle of 8

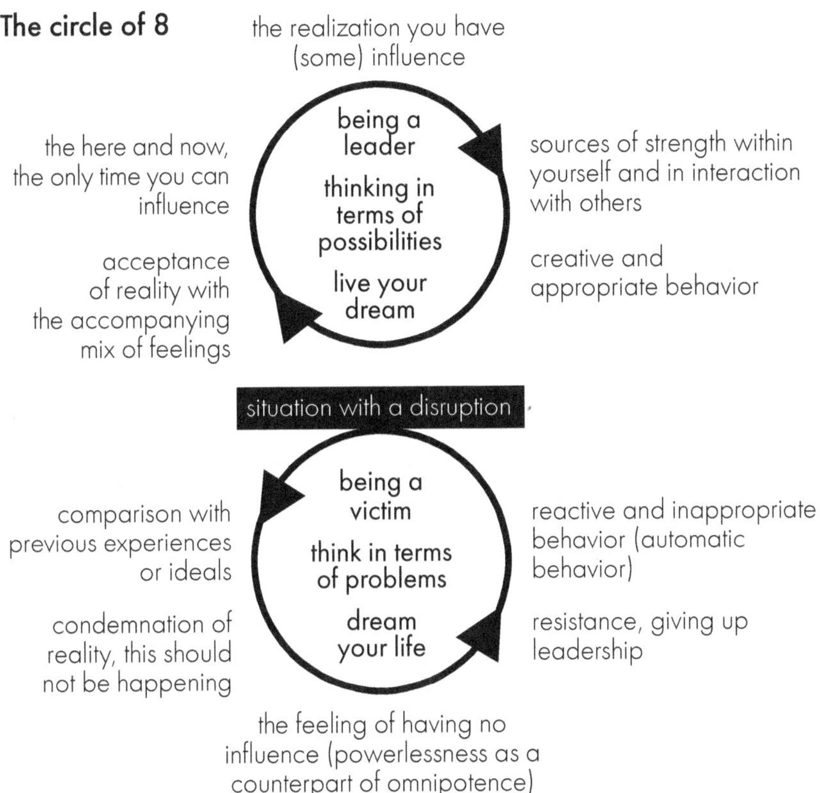

The lower circle shows the victim role. When something goes wrong, people may think in terms of problems, feel powerless, and exhibit reactive and inadequate behavior. Once they have done that, they move up and think in terms of possibilities.

The lower circle is allowed but not required. Without denying the feeling that arises in the lower circle, moving to the upper circle is possible, which is necessary if things should change. The only time that can be influenced is the here and now. People can tap into sources of strength in themselves or others. "What is possible? What can I do?" They then demonstrate personal leadership: thinking in terms of possibilities.

You dream your life in the lower circle and live your dream in the upper circle.

What I find important in this model is that it says "acceptance of reality *with the mix of associated feelings.*" The feelings in the lower circle are real. I advise my clients to recognize, acknowledge, and feel those feelings. Hiding these feelings can work against people, but they shouldn't be allowed to get in the way either. I advise my clients to give their feelings the space they need but also to focus on following through. People can complete the lower circle in just a few seconds or a whole day when they experience a major setback. But do follow through after that!

Evaluation

The third phase of self-management is evaluation. How did it go? Was the agreed plan followed? Were adjustments needed? Which lessons were learned, and what new intentions exist? This phase is easier to execute if learning or research objectives are defined beforehand, providing a clear reference point to evaluate. Unfocused actions – unintentional actions due to seeing it at once – have no prior objective and usually don't need evaluation. But in that case, someone no longer learns from experience.

Mindset

Many gifted people have to be careful that evaluation does not have a destructive effect by letting negativity and self-blame take over. This is counterproductive. As a universal rule, people always know more afterward than they could have known beforehand. Gifted people who tend not to get started until they have 100 percent certainty do not cope well with setbacks or opposition during execution. They are also negative in their evaluation: things should have gone differently, and they blame themselves and/or others for this. They hold onto the ideal picture in their mind, which gets in the way of learning. Often these are people with a fixed mindset, a term from Carol Dweck's mindset theory. I try to help these clients develop a more growth-oriented mindset in my coaching. I write more about this in Chapter 4.

Reflection

Another important part of evaluation involves using deeper information processing, the most important characteristic of high sensitivity. More about this later. Evaluating the past day with yourself leads to new insights, creative ideas, and good intentions for the future. I try to teach my clients that they should spend at least half an hour every day reflecting in an imaginary hammock. It is an essential part of self-management.

Journal exercises

I give my clients journal assignments to analyze situations on a daily basis. Ideally, they should write something every day, but at least three times a week. The assignment lets my clients analyze situations around a particular theme in their lives. Recording this information for several weeks gives them information in which they can identify patterns. Once they recognize these patterns, my clients often change their behavior immediately. If my clients do not know how to organize such a journal themselves, I offer them some basic questions to get started. "When and how did the theme manifest itself? Describe the situation." "What did you think? What did you feel? What did you do?" "How did the other person react? What effect did this have on you?" etc.

Understanding thoughts and feelings

Another tool for getting out of a bad time is to list one's thoughts and feelings. I started using this tool to treat fear of failure.

A gifted person can approach a subject from multiple perspectives and at various levels of abstraction. This approach also applies to their multifaceted feeling. Multiple levels of abstraction and perspectives evoke different emotions. Gifted people feel many things at the same time. Their complexity of thought is also seen in the way they feel. Using the tool I developed, a client analyses a specific situation. This could be a situation in the future when it comes to fear of failure or a difficult decision, but it is also useful to evaluate situations from the past.

Describe the subject or situation and make lists.
• What are the negative thoughts?
• What negative feelings are there?
• What are the neutral thoughts?
• Were there also neutral feelings?
• What about positive thoughts?
• And positive feelings?

Filling in this outline helps gifted people understand the
complexity of their thoughts and feelings. The advantage of
visually working this out is that the client can look at it from
a certain distance. "It's a lot to deal with, so it's normal that I
find/found this difficult." The client can use the final result to
determine what they consider important. Or, in the process of
choosing, they can decide what they want to go for.
The client can also weigh the importance of a feeling or thought.

Analysis for complex thinkers and feelers

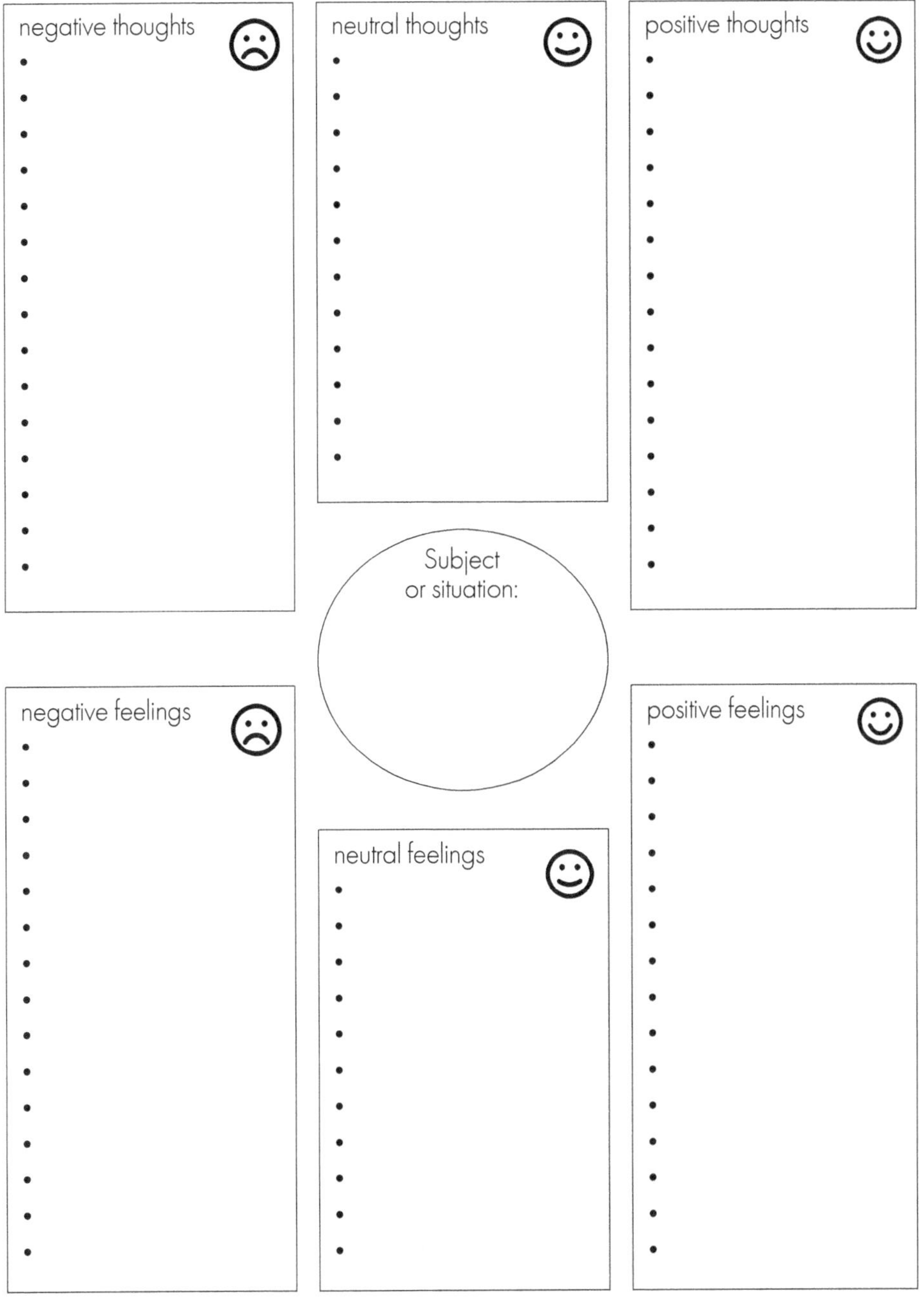

Focus on positive feelings

A gifted person can try to focus on positive feelings, for example, by letting joy prevail over frustration. The feeling of frustration may exist but shouldn't be allowed to take over. Or, if it concerns a situation in the future, they can determine whether their courage is greater than their fears. If the courage is greater, they can face the situation. If this is not the case, it is good to leave it for a while. Adjusting the goal is a better option in that case. Negative feelings are normal. They are there for a reason. If these feelings aren't acknowledged, they can take on a life of their own.

2.5. Highly sensitive

According to the Delphi Model of Giftedness, gifted people are highly sensitive in their perception. Many of my clients' problems are related to this high sensitivity. One example is their sensitivity to rejection. The weight of these experiences manifests itself when a gifted person feels rejected if someone so much as raises an eyebrow.

In 2016, Professor Elke Van Hoof and I conducted a study into the relationship between giftedness and high sensitivity in adults. Our research revealed that 87 percent of gifted people are also highly sensitive. A similar study conducted by the Erasmus University in cooperation with the IHBV in 2018 found a percentage of 77.

Thus, many gifted people are also highly sensitive, but like giftedness, high sensitivity manifests itself differently in everyone. To make my clients care for themselves properly, they must understand what high sensitivity is and how it works for them as individuals. Self-care and stress reduction vary from one person to another. Some people benefit from listening to classical music, some take a bath, and others find peace through meditation. I instruct my clients to make their own high sensitivity profile, which they can use to figure out the best way to take care of themselves. I also work on emotion regulation with my clients. I write more about this in paragraph 4.2 on emotional intelligence.

An explanation

Aron & Aron published an article on Sensory Processing Sensitivity in 1997 and defined the following characteristics, abbreviated with the acronym DOES:

1. **depth** of information processing
2. easily **overstimulated**
3. **emotional** reactivity
4. sensing the **subtle**

In addition, according to this study, high sensitivity is innate and occurs in 15 to 20 percent of humanity. According to Aron, it is a categorical fact: you are either highly sensitive or you are not. It has a genetic basis and is localized in the central nervous system. There is increasing scientific interest in high sensitivity. Professor Elke Van Hoof is a clinical psychologist. She studies high sensitivity and wrote the popular science book *Hoogsensitief* (*Highly Sensitive*). The research she and I conducted together is also briefly described in that book. In her book, Van Hoof distinguishes between high sensitivity and hypersensitivity.

high sensitivity	hypersensitivity
• ability to absorb large amounts of information from the environment • depth of information processing	• overstimulation • emotionality
• perception and processing	• responsiveness

Van Hoof states that the most important characteristics of high sensitivity lie in perception and processing, which can lead to hypersensitive responses.

Not all highly sensitive people react in a hypersensitive way. Some people have developed skills to prevent overstimulation, and other people have such highly developed emotion regulation that even strong emotions are not visible to the outside world. Conversely, not every overstimulation or emotional outburst is due to high sensitivity. Anyone can become overstimulated when exposed to too many stimuli for too long.

Van Hoof refers to overstimulation and emotionality as 'hypersensitivity.' Van Hoof's use of this word caused some commotion in the Netherlands, where the Dutch words *hooggevoeligheid* ('hypersensitivity') and *hoogsensitiviteit* ('high sensitivity') are used synonymously. In a joint communiqué, the term *overgevoelig* ('overly sensitive') was later chosen for the responsive side. I disagree with this choice because that word has a negative connotation and is something highly sensitive people are regularly accused of by others. I prefer the term 'highly or strongly responsive.'

What is nice about the distinction made by Van Hoof is that it creates space for developing skills to better deal with high sensitivity. This way, a highly sensitive person can benefit more from the advantages of high sensitivity and be less affected by the negative aspects. What I work on with my clients is helping them view their high sensitivity as a strength, particularly in combination with their high intelligence, and how to use it.

Positive aspects

I teach my clients to be aware of the positive aspects of being highly sensitive. In the many workshops I give on this subject, we always make a list in a plenary setting.

According to my clients, the advantages of being highly sensitive are:
- being able to enjoy things intensely
- being able to sense situations well (usually before others)
- knowing what people need
- being able to make astute (nuanced) analyses
- demonstrating exemplary behavior
- being approachable to people; others often confide in you with their problems

2.6. Gender identity (androgyny)

Many gifted people do not fall within the average regarding gender. The stereotypical male and female traits do not apply to them. Gifted women have above-average intelligence, a trait that is considered "masculine" in our culture and often viewed as cold, distant, and analytical. The same applies to gifted men. They have above-average "feminine" traits, namely the warm, empathic, and sensitive side. Many gifted women are not really girly, and many gifted men are not particularly macho. Animus and Anima appear to be more balanced in gifted individuals than non-gifted people of the same gender. Unfortunately, there is no solid scientific research on this yet.

Based on what I see in practice, gifted people do not seem to have a strong sense of gender. I also think that sex change is more common among gifted people than non-gifted people, but I do not have any hard data. The same applies to bisexuality. I often hear my clients say, "I'm not attracted to someone's gender but to their personality."
P. Susan Jackson is the founder and director of the Daimon Institute, which focuses on the exceptionally gifted (IQ 160+). She has developed the *Integral practice for the gifted* model to provide guidance to her clients. In this model, Jackson describes gender development as one of the nine developmental lines of a gifted individual.

James T. Webb's book on misdiagnoses of gifted people also includes a section on gender identity in relation to giftedness. He refers to studies by Barbara Kerr in 1997, 2001, and 2015, in which she found that gifted boys and girls are more androgynous than the average population and that this often leads to gender identity issues.

Gifted men and women rarely find recognition when discussing this topic with non-gifted people of the same gender. Clients affected by this feel a great sense of relief when I explain that many other gifted people experience the same issues. Depending on the intensity of the problem, I may refer them to professionals who specialize in this area.

2.7. Creation styles

How do gifted people create? Ronald T. Kellogg characterized two styles of creation. He compared these to the composers Beethoven and Mozart and named the styles after them. Beethoven and Mozart had different approaches to composing music. The results of their work prove that neither approach is better than the other but that there are major differences between their creation styles.

The Beethoven style
Beethoven was a hard, disciplined worker. He went to his workplace every morning and came back home every evening. He would play a little music, write a little, play some more, cross things out, improve and adjust what he'd written, and start the whole process again. Beethoven's hard work was measurable and well-organized. It was measurable in terms of hours and well-organized because everyone knew where he was. At the end of the day, he would stop working, leave his room, and go and do other things. The next day would be the same. And after a certain amount of time, this process resulted in a phenomenal piece of music.

The Mozart style

Mozart had a very different way of working. He was busy with anything and everything. He was lively, happy-go-lucky, and seemed to focus on what he liked without worrying about his work. But Mozart was always composing in his mind. When he had a eureka moment, in which he finished the piece of music in his mind, he would lock himself in his study and wouldn't come out again until he had put the result down on paper. Mozart wrote out his scores in one go, without crossing anything out and without stopping to eat. He needed to empty his mind. This style also resulted in a brilliant piece of music. Much of Mozart's working process was not visible to the outside world.

Beethoven style	Mozart style
Creation process outside the person	Creation process within the person
Needs intermediate sketches/ visualizations to progress, builds up in parts	Plans, coordinates, "composes" in their mind, works from a whole
Easy to work with: • You see that they are working • You know what they are working on • Produces intermediate products, so the status is known • Influencing/adjustment possible along the way, feedback is incorporated • Criticism isn't taken poorly, as the product is incomplete in their own eyes • Sharing intermediate products also creates support	*Challenging to work with:* • You don't see that they are working • You think they are busy doing something else • Status/progress unknown • You have to hope they will complete the work on time • Influencing/adjustment virtually impossible along the way • No intermediate products meaning no/little coordination or support is created • Does not share until finished: criticism/feedback is taken very personally

Both composers produced high-quality pieces of music, but it seems as if Beethoven worked much harder than Mozart ever did. But all is not as it seems. People could not see that Mozart was working, but that doesn't mean he wasn't working. Both styles lead to a good result in their own way.

When working with others, people in today's society expect the Beethoven style. It is good to see that people are working and to see and discuss the interim progress, especially if a deadline has been set. It facilitates control, idea sharing, and adjustment, making it possible to share interim results with others. In the case of the Mozart style, people have to assume that things will turn out all right. They don't know how far a Mozart is, and when it's finished, it's finished. There is no opportunity to contribute ideas or make adjustments. A Mozart will often take criticism of the final product personally.
Almost all of my clients identify with the Mozart style. As expected, they encounter problems because of it, especially when dealing with colleagues.

Knowing about these two creation styles helps make it possible to do something with them. When gifted people are aware of their preferred style, they use it. If they use the Mozart style, they may express their views on things they are certain of. Another person, whether gifted or not, will know that it is being worked on and will be fine.

Another problem for people with a Mozart style is that the actual hours they work are less visible, also for themselves because they often do not charge for these hours. They only keep track of or invoice the visibly productive hours, even though there would have been no final result without the preliminary process. In addition, gifted people with a Mozart style who lack a positive self-image may struggle with their preconceived ideas. They label all the "non-productive" hours as idle, procrastination, laziness, or other judgments. Knowledge of the Mozart style ensures that gifted people can become more optimistic about their work attitude and view themselves more positively.

The diamond

A tool called the diamond is available for this process of creation by gifted people.

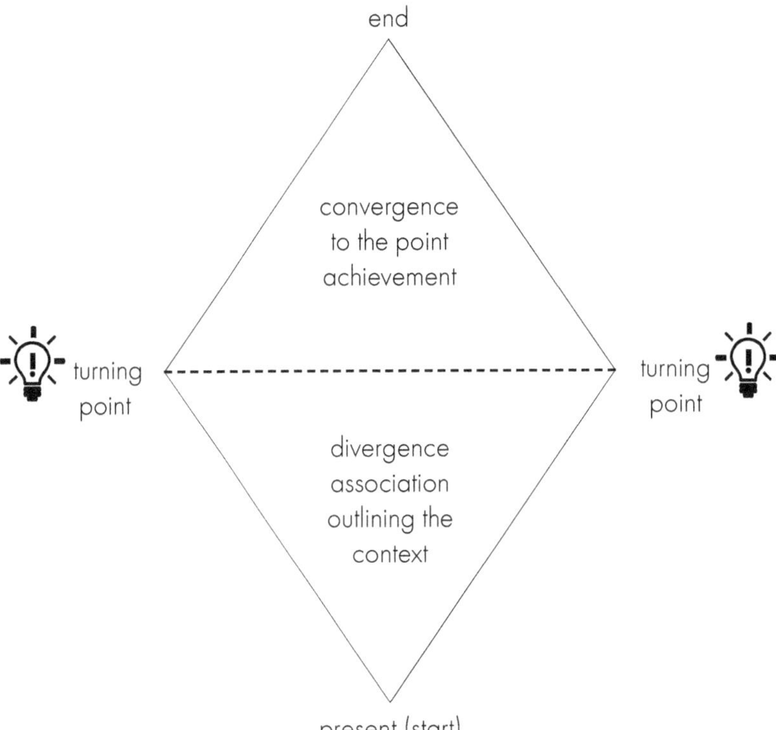

This diamond explains how the creation process works and at what stage the gifted person is. Knowledge and understanding of this process help gifted people themselves as well as their non-gifted colleagues or bystanders. The starting point is at the bottom of the diamond. From there, the gifted person enlarges the context and, as shown, reaches a bend somewhere in the middle. This bend fits with the eureka feeling I referred to in relation to the Mozart style, the moment when the gifted person sees how it works. From that overall image, the gifted person starts to converge and heads straight to the end goal. Gifted people are good at both processes.

The bend is delayed when a gifted person suffers from fear of failure. Uncertainty causes them to involve more and more, making the image much bigger and more complex and delaying the bend and the transition to achievement. A deadline can force the gifted person to choose, usually resulting in little satisfaction and a negative opinion of one's performance. When a client fails to get started and remains stuck in not knowing even with deadlines looming, there may be other issues. This avoidance behavior is sometimes caused by a traumatic experience, in which case referral to another mental health professional is recommended.

I have to teach many of my clients how to cope with their Mozart style. I teach them to take a bird's-eye view of their work and ask questions about their process: What am I already certain about? What can I tell my colleagues and manager now so that they also know I am working on it and how far along I am? What do I need to get to the bend? What can I do to gain more certainty? Can my goals be broken down into smaller pieces? What is stopping me? What information do I need? What am I uncertain about?

Of course, this does not mean that there aren't any gifted people who prefer the Beethoven style. I know many gifted people who work at universities and can work and experiment in a very structured and detailed manner without encountering many problems.

Processing

Once they know about their giftedness, many things start falling into place for my clients. They suddenly understand many things. This knowledge thus provides a sense of relief but can also initiate a grieving process about what has happened and what they never understood.

3.1. Coaching - psychotherapy

Coaching is a different profession than psychotherapy. I am a coach, not a psychotherapist. I do not treat psychiatric conditions but coach people in discovering and managing their giftedness. The knowledge about giftedness that I provide in my coaching processes leads to recognition and acknowledgment, giving my clients room to breathe. This enables my clients to take action. Although I do not provide therapy in a medical sense, many of my clients experience a healing, therapeutic effect from our sessions. This means that my coaching goes deep enough to help a client move forward, although some clients may also continue to experience major obstacles without a change occurring. There is often more going on in such cases, such as more severe forms of trauma. I refer such cases to a psychotherapist. They may need EMDR or other forms of trauma therapy, and I am not trained to provide those. Fortunately, I have an extensive network of professionals to whom I can refer my clients.

3.2. Cumulative relational trauma, rejection sensitivity

High standards

As humans, we tend to base things on our personal perspective. Without realizing it, we impose our standards on the rest of the world and view the world as if other people were the same as us. Unfortunately, things often go wrong when gifted people see themselves as the norm. It suits gifted people to take ownership of their qualities and recognize that they have developed certain skills more strongly than average.

Taking ownership of your qualities

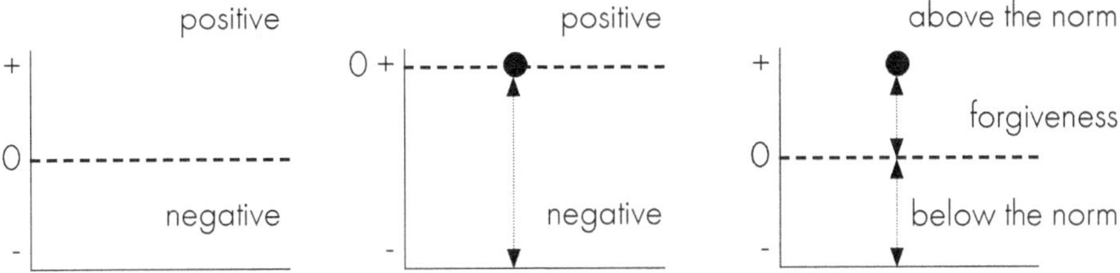

These three diagrams show what I mean by taking ownership of your qualities. The first diagram shows the presence of a norm. Everything above the norm is regarded as more positive, and everything below is viewed as more negative. When someone has a characteristic above the norm, and that is their point of reference, as shown in the second diagram, that person will experience that very few others are above that norm while many people are below it. Many gifted people do this without realizing it. For example, gifted people quickly see solutions to problems and grasp complex situations. They then assume that everyone sees things their way. But they see solutions earlier than others because of their high intelligence, of which they may not be aware. Thus, gifted people unintentionally impose their high standards on others. Their standards are not realistic, and they may become angry or disappointed when others do not live up to their expectations. However, it is not unwillingness on the other person's part, nor are they necessarily stupid or slow. Still, in the gifted person's perception, the other person deviates from their projected expectations.
The third diagram shows some space forming between the gifted person and the norm and that the area is not entirely negative. This area creates more room for patience and forgiveness of others, such as colleagues at work.

Little "t" trauma

I see cumulative microtrauma in many clients, also called cumulative relational trauma (little "t" trauma). This type of trauma is not based on a single traumatic event like a roadside bomb or rape. Cumulative microtrauma consists of many small traumas. It is as if thousands of waterdrops fall into a bucket until it overflows. A drop falls into the bucket whenever a gifted person feels unheard, unseen, misunderstood, or not taken seriously. Disproportionate responses occur when the bucket is full; a new drop causes the bucket to overflow. It is about recognition, being seen or heard, being allowed to exist, being good enough, and being accepted. While growing up, most gifted adults were not recognized or acknowledged as a gifted child (in the Netherlands).

The nuanced nature of their experiences also means that they do not have the same experience of reciprocity that many non-gifted people have. That means that mini-traumas accumulate from an early age. And it is this accumulation that can result in serious trauma. This is a common theme among gifted adults, but the intensity and scope vary from one client to another. Sometimes this leads to symptoms of post-traumatic stress. In such cases, I refer my clients to a psychotherapist.

Rejection sensitivity

High sensitivity can amplify rejection sensitivity, turning it into a self-fulfilling prophecy. The brain always looks for confirmation of expectations. The perception then focuses on even more rejection. A simple frown can be interpreted as a rejection. The brain becomes hypervigilant and is thus highly sensitive to potentially dangerous environmental triggers, which our brain would not normally perceive as dangerous.

Very often, just being aware of this is enough for my clients. Knowing that it exists is enough to reduce its adverse effects. In some cases, the consequences of the microtrauma may be too great for the individual concerned to take action on their own. If that is the case, I refer the client to a specialized therapist.

Self-esteem and self-confidence grow when clients start working with this knowledge. Their higher self-esteem and sense of self-confidence help reduce fear. Taking ownership of their share helps clients interpret microsignals differently. Simply acknowledging their part in the interpretation often leads to more proportionate responses.

Bullying in the workplace

The gap between gifted and non-gifted people often becomes apparent when behavior is misinterpreted. If a non-gifted manager or colleague does not do what a gifted person expects, this is not necessarily due to negative intentions; it can also mean that the gifted person has set the bar too high.

If the gifted person is not aware of this difference, they may believe their manager or colleague is bullying them. Projection can play a role in that case. When the gifted person views themselves as the norm and expects another person to exhibit the same high degree of empathy, they risk disappointment.

A gifted person may then have thoughts like: "I would never do that to another person!" or "Don't you see what's happening? Do something about it!" Because a non-gifted person may not have the same degree of empathy, they may overlook the seriousness of the situation and will not intervene. This can turn the non-gifted person into the culprit in the gifted person's eyes. The gifted person must become aware of their share in the situation. The following questions can help: Is it about my experience or the culprit's intentions? Am I being bullied, or do I feel like I'm being bullied? Could there be a different explanation? Is the other person really aware of what they're doing? Or am I projecting my greater consciousness onto the other person?

It is often a matter of inability rather than unwillingness. Hanlon's Razor ties in with this: "Never attribute to malice that which can be adequately explained by stupidity." This statement should not be taken too seriously. Stupidity is referred to in jest here and does not align with how I view equality and equivalence.

Psychiatrist and psychologist Kazimierz Dabrowski studied personality development, particularly in gifted people. The average person's identity is shaped by and in the environment in which they grow up. From a Dabrowskian perspective, group norms and values that also shape people's personalities originate there. The feeling of being "us" is created in groups. People who deviate from an implicit or explicit group norm do not contribute to the feeling of being "us" and are thus pushed out, sometimes automatically. This can be done through bullying and exclusion. Afterward, it may turn out that the system cannot function without a target, and the bullied person is then replaced with someone else so that the group can continue. This is called scapegoating. People need to be excluded to determine the group norm. The extremes are excluded so that the average is restored. Bullying serves a purpose on a group dynamic level. This also occurs in groups of gifted people when they joke about someone else. It is a form of bonding within the group, which increases group cohesion.

Bullying appears to have a functional value for the group but also says a lot about safety, connectivity, and inclusion within the group. Bullying harms the bullied person, even if the feeling of being bullied only exists in the bullied person's perception and the culprits have no deliberate intention of bullying.

3.3. Imposter syndrome

When a gifted person comes up with a solution without much effort and people still respond with great enthusiasm, this can feel surreal to that person. They may get the impression that others think they have done more than they did. This feeling can make them feel anxious and afraid of being found out. Hence the name: imposter syndrome. Albert Einstein is the most famous and incredible example of someone who experienced this syndrome. Because of his intelligence, Einstein easily stepped in when someone presented him with a problem, and he would then come up with at least a partial solution. Everyone responded enthusiastically without Einstein himself understanding what all the fuss was about. He hadn't had to put in any effort at all, so he didn't feel like having done anything. He found the audience's response exaggerated and perhaps even somewhat embarrassing. Even Einstein was afraid of eventually being found out by a real expert.

Many gifted people in my practice are affected by this syndrome to some extent. They do not see their added value or do not rate it highly enough. They conclude that they just did something without a plan, so they wonder what it is all about.

You often hear of the following:
- People with *little* experience or knowledge about a particular subject *overestimate* their knowledge and ability and are *quick* to call themselves experts.
- People with *a lot* of experience or knowledge about a particular subject *underestimate* their knowledge and ability and *rarely* call themselves experts.

This phenomenon is called the Dunning-Kruger effect. It is named after psychologists David Dunning and Justin Kruger, who studied it.

Gifted people often belong to the second group and usually see through the first category easily. The latter may explain why they are slow to call themselves experts. It suits gifted people to make their added value explicit by examining it.

3.4. Afraid to shine

Being afraid to shine is the fear of achieving goals. Often, it is a fear of the consequences of being successful. Many of my clients suffer from this to a greater or lesser extent.

Being afraid to shine often involves low self-esteem and a high degree of empathy. Because of their low self-esteem, the gifted person does not dare to thrive. Because of their high degree of empathy, the gifted person does not want to outshine someone else. In addition, this is influenced by the expectations of others – perhaps exaggerated by the spotlights – and certainly the gifted person's expectations. This fear increases by the idea of having to accomplish too great an achievement and not being able to do so, or of being able to achieve something but not being able to deal with the consequences.

Making this mechanism transparent can help. I show my clients how abstract thinking is involved and what role they play in this themselves.

The before-during-after outline can help tackle the fear of shining. We consider the problem, what was done, what happened, and what was achieved.

Many of my clients have demonstrated that their colleagues do not perform as well as they do at work by unintentionally outshining them. How? Simply by being themselves, working hard, and achieving good results. However, those around them don't always appreciate this. When clients experience this repeatedly, they can also become afraid to shine. I let these clients read Marianne Williamson's beautiful poem, *Our Deepest Fear*.

Our deepest fear is not that we are inadequate,
Our deepest fear is that we are powerful beyond measure.
It is our light and not our darkness that most frightens us.
We ask ourselves:
Who am I to be brilliant, gorgeous, talented and fabulous?
Actually, who are you not to be?
You are a child of God.
There's nothing enlightened about shrinking,
so that other people won't feel insecure around you.
We are meant to shine as children do.
We were born to manifest the glory of God that is within us.
It is not just in one of us.
It is in everyone.
As we let our own light shine,
we unconsciously give other people permission to do the same.
As we are liberated from our fear,
our presence automatically liberates others.

Marianne Williamson uit 'A return to love' (1992)

3.5. Low self-esteem

Manja de Neef wrote a self-help book for people with low self-esteem. The book entitled *Negatief zelfbeeld* (*Negative Self-image*) describes a path the reader can take to actively improve their self-esteem. This self-help book is also widely used in psychotherapy and group therapy in the Netherlands.

Low self-esteem, or a negative self-image, never fully disappears. But placing a positive image alongside it can balance it out. For some clients, their low self-esteem can best be described as a box filled with negative experiences; others even have closets full of these boxes. Clients' perceptions become colored by this. They keep seeking and storing reinforcement of their negative self-image. It is a self-fulfilling prophecy. Self-esteem needs validation. Therefore, De Neef encourages people to consciously collect positive experiences to provide balance. An additional effect of this assignment is that when people know they have to write down three positive experiences one evening, they will actively seek out those positive experiences. This automatically gives clients a more positive perception.

When my clients want to work on their self-esteem, I sometimes use exercises from the book, such as listing positive qualities and collecting positive experiences in a journal.

It is a nice, general method not explicitly aimed at gifted people. In her book, De Neef recognizes the added value of having a "buddy" to keep going. She advises the reader to find someone with whom they can discuss the process regularly. I also encourage this and prefer that my clients find someone to take on this role in their own environment. I am prepared to take on this role only if a client is unable to find a suitable person in their surroundings. In that case, the process takes considerably longer than the usual coaching process with me.

My only reservation about De Neef's book concerns the chapter about high standards and perfectionism. This works differently for non-gifted people than for gifted people and uses different yardsticks. The usual yardsticks do not include the talents of gifted people. A gifted person can think more steps ahead and thus has greater ambition. This ambition should not be dismissed as too high because the higher standards are indeed feasible for a gifted person.

Therefore, the yardstick is not always valid or valid for everyone. The yardstick used for non-gifted people is not the same as for gifted people and vice versa. A non-gifted person's ambition is just different from that of a gifted person.

Unfortunately, this book is not available in English. But maybe a similar method to work on self-esteem is available in your country.

Shame

Shame is another common theme among gifted people with low self-esteem. Brené Brown is a research professor of social work at the University of Houston specializing in shame and vulnerability. Her TEDtalks are very beneficial when working on low self-esteem. They help my clients broaden their perspective, enabling them to practice with this material.

3.6. Referral

When I have clients with a possible trauma, I usually refer them to professionals who exhibit many characteristics of giftedness and are knowledgeable about it. There is a good reason for this: it takes one to know one. Being able to follow the quick and complex thinking of a gifted client is a prerequisite for being able to help or guide that person properly. Any possible disapproval of this way of thinking should also be avoided. I know of upsetting examples of gifted clients reliving part of their trauma in group therapy, surrounded by non-gifted people and a non-gifted therapist. What led them to seek help in the first place recurs during therapy. This is damaging because the gifted person again experiences rejection, lack of understanding, or exclusion in a setting that should have been healing and safe. I have many psychologists, psychotherapists, and a few psychiatrists in my network who are familiar with the theme of 'giftedness,' to whom I can refer my clients. Often, a client will come back to me afterward to complete the coaching process. These contacts in my network also refer many clients to me, for example, when career issues remain after therapy.

I am regularly asked whether a mental health professional for gifted people must be gifted themselves. As stated above, it is very beneficial if a mental health professional can keep up with the client's pace, complexity, and intensity. But simply keeping up is not enough. A gifted client switches gears between different levels of experience and consciousness simultaneously. The mental health professional must be able to connect on all these levels for the client to feel seen, heard, and understood.

Feeling of rejection

Sometimes a client will experience my referral more as a personal rejection than as help. They may feel abandoned or rejected. The client's reaction then often fits in with the issue at hand.
That bothers me for a while because I want the best for my clients. I do not view this as my failure but as recognizing where my profession ends and another begins. Peer consultation and supervision help me reflect on my performance.

3.7. Misdiagnoses, dual, and missed diagnoses

Many of my clients have a history of using mental health services. Unfortunately, because knowledge about giftedness is not yet widespread, giftedness is regularly overlooked or considered irrelevant during the diagnostic assessment. To assess behavior that could be attributed to giftedness, psychiatrists and therapists use the Diagnostic and Statistical Manual of Mental Disorders, 5th Edition (DSM-V®), the manual for categorizing and defining symptoms, problems, and disorders. Common diagnoses that can be misdiagnosed in combination with giftedness include attention deficit disorder (ADD), attention deficit hyperactivity disorder (ADHD), autism spectrum disorder, bipolar disorder, and obsessive-compulsive disorder (OCD).
Diagnoses may also be missed if a gifted person uses their intelligence to influence the results of questionnaires and masks specific behaviors in interviews with the therapist.
As stated above, this is not my area of expertise, and I am therefore cautious when making claims related to diagnostics. Because more research and knowledge are needed on this subject, a national knowledge network on psychiatry and giftedness was recently

launched in the Netherlands. Unfortunately, there are too many harrowing cases of inappropriate treatment and medication.

The book *Misdiagnosis and Dual Diagnoses of Gifted Children and Adults: ADHD, Bipolar, OCD, Asperger's, Depression, and Other Disorders* (second edition) by James T. Webb et al. is essential for improving knowledge on this subject. In my opinion, this book should be compulsory reading for psychologists, psychotherapists, and psychiatrists. More knowledge about giftedness is desperately needed in mental health care.

Growing

In this chapter, I describe how to work with clients to change their behavior. Earlier, it became evident that insight can be enough to bring about change: once clients understand how something works, they can quickly put it into practice. But gifted people also need to rehearse different behavior.

After the grieving period caused by learning about their giftedness and how it has impacted their lives, many clients experience a release of energy. They develop a new self-image, and their prospects change. This also requires new skills. Often, more opportunities open up to them than they had ever imagined.

4.1. Mindset

Carol Dweck studies the subject of mindset, and her work is also popular in the world of giftedness. She defines mindset as "a set of beliefs or a way of thinking that determines one's behavior, outlook and mental attitude." In other words, beliefs influence thoughts, and thoughts influence actions, which influence results. The results reinforce beliefs, completing the circle.

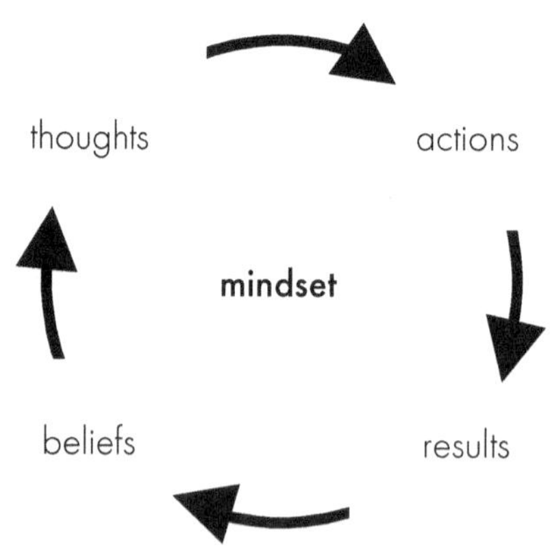

Dweck discovered that people differ in how they think about themselves and, in particular, about their intelligence and qualities. From this, she distilled a *fixed* mindset and a *growth* mindset.

Someone with a fixed mindset believes that their personal characteristics are fixed. People are born with a certain "amount" of intelligence and qualities, which they use for the rest of their lives.

Someone with a growth mindset believes that they can continue to develop. Innate ability is the starting point from which someone grows by working hard and gaining experience.

Fixed mindset (wants to appear smart)	Growth mindset (wants to learn)
Avoids challenges	Takes on challenges
Gives up quickly when faced with obstacles	Keeps going despite obstacles
Sees effort as pointless	Sees effort as the path to mastery
Ignores meaningful feedback	Learns from criticism
Feels threatened by the success of others	Is inspired by the success of others

Here too, two extremes are placed side by side, but the reality is not so black and white. Sometimes a continuum is mentioned, in which someone has a fixed mindset in one area and a growth mindset in another.

The development of a growth mindset involves four steps:
1. Being aware of thoughts: learning to hear the voice of the fixed mindset.
2. Realizing that there is a choice: knowing that new skills can be achieved through focused effort.
3. Challenging these thoughts: responding with a growth mindset.
4. Putting it into practice outside the comfort zone: taking small steps and celebrating progress.

Many of my clients have a fixed mindset. This mindset can prevent them from doing things they want to do. Once they know about this theory, many of my clients wish to develop a more growth-oriented mindset. I don't believe that someone with a fixed mindset can completely replace it with a growth mindset, but I do think the fixed mindset can be made less dominant by placing a healthy voice alongside it. This requires a constructive inner dialogue.

The fear associated with the fixed mindset does not simply disappear. Clients will need to step out of their comfort zone and take one or more risks. It involves recognizing and acknowledging the fear that is released and learning to deal with it. It's good when things get tense or slightly more than tense. That's healthy. But if the tension turns to panic, even mild panic, it is better to find a less risky alternative. Panic is unhealthy tension that is best avoided, not least because it eventually increases the fear of leaving the comfort zone and taking risks. It becomes more challenging to get over the panic, and that panic is there for a reason. I work with my clients to figure out what's best for them. What does panic mean? And I let them take smaller steps. But I also stress that if they want to grow and learn, they have to step out of their comfort zone!

However, if it doesn't work, it doesn't work. A person can only cope with so much tension. Clients have to find their growth zone, but they should do so in small steps. It is also important to set realistic goals. Not everything is achievable, and not everything is malleable. Many clients blame themselves if they fail. We reflect during the coaching sessions, and I encourage them to try again, using a different approach if necessary.

So here, too, clients can learn through experience that a growth process is going on. Clients can learn through experience and make adjustments where necessary. This enables them to develop an alternative strategy.

After Senninger (2000)

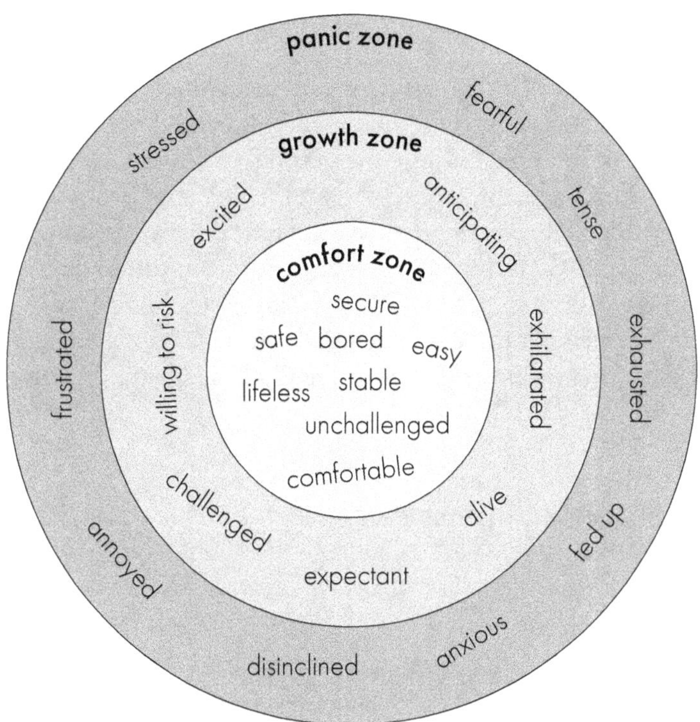

Comfort zone	Growth zone	Panic zone
No challenge No stress	Quite a challenge A little bit of stress	Huge challenge High level of stress
Limited need to think/prepare	Requires some real thinking/preparation	Cognitive overload
Limited learning	Effective learning	Limited learning

Dweck also studied the role of compliments relating to mindset. Praising the process and effort stimulates the growth mindset. But a compliment on intelligence will not have that effect, according to Dweck.

Regarding types of compliments, American psychologist Sally Reis states that gifted girls should be complimented on their intelligence more often because they then feel it is okay for women to be intelligent.

Dweck's work has been criticized because it is strongly based on malleability, as if you can achieve anything as long as you work hard enough. However, not everything is feasible or desirable for everyone. Remember the CoreTalents and the fact that gifted people should focus their energy on their strong CoreTalents, the energizers.

4.2. Emotional intelligence

"Anyone can become angry... That is easy. But to be angry
with the right person,
to the right degree,
at the right time,
for the right purpose,
and in the right way,
that is not for everyone, nor is it easy."

Aristotle

A misconception about giftedness is that someone with high cognitive intelligence (IQ) must have low emotional intelligence (EQ). This has been proven false (by J. Derksen, among others). IQ is often used as an abbreviation for cognitive intelligence and EQ for emotional intelligence. Both cases refer to a measured intelligence.

However, the concepts are very different: IQ is relatively static and is about innate ability, while EQ is a developmental concept and is about skills. Studies investigating the relationship between the two show that IQ and EQ are not strongly correlated.

Emotional skills are important. When gifted people grow up in an environment with little understanding of (the intensity of) their emotions while being rewarded for intellectual skills, they will be more likely to trust rationality than feelings.
It is also possible that a child has experienced such intense pain that they decide they don't want to feel anything anymore and shut down the feeling. I have clients who remember precisely when that happened.

What is emotional intelligence?

Emotional intelligence is a set of emotional and social skills that together determine how we:
• perceive and express ourselves
• develop and maintain social relationships
• deal with challenges
• use emotional information in an effective and meaningful way

The importance of emotional intelligence

Emotional intelligence is important for everyone, not just for gifted people. Everyone has emotions, which influence our behavior, actions, effectiveness, and well-being.
When people manage their emotions effectively, they make better decisions, cope with stress more easily, and can form and maintain stronger relationships.

Behavior can be seen as a formula with multiple variables. Emotion is also a variable that influences how people behave. Gifted people who have "shut down" their feelings – often in childhood – do not include their feelings in their behavioral choices. This is not sustainable. Emotions are essential for everyone, and shutting them down will eventually affect a person's well-being and often the people around them.

Many of the coaching needs I see in my practice are related to emotional intelligence and emotional skills, such as:

- balance between emotions and rational thinking
- dealing with criticism and opposition better
- getting better at social interaction, such as with colleagues, and also with managers (authority)
- improving communication skills, particularly the desire to be better understood
- high sensitivity: sensing other people's emotions
- low self-esteem

Testing EQ

In the 1980s, American-Israeli psychologist Reuven Bar-On was the first to develop a test to measure emotional intelligence (EQ). Based on this test, Howard Gardner, a psychologist at Harvard University, incorporated emotional intelligence into a theory of multiple intelligences. Later, in the 1990s, psychologists John Mayer and Peter Salovey developed an extensive EQ test. Psychologist Daniel Goleman made the subject popular and practical for business purposes.

The Reuven Bar-On test was given a 2.0 makeover in 2011. MHS, a Canadian company specializing in assessments, later made this questionnaire more widely applicable, enabling non-psychologists to administer the test, provided they have received the relevant training. I took this training course in 2018, which qualified me to administer the revised Bar-On EQ-i 2.0 test.

Measuring EQ is never a goal in itself. It is a tool that can provide insight into particular issues. However, the test creators did make the concept similar to an IQ test. The two tests even have the same average score of 100. An EQ (or IQ) score of 130 means that someone is two standard deviations removed from the mean and that this person is highly emotionally intelligent. Yet IQ remains an entirely different concept from EQ. IQ is assumed to measure innate ability. The EQ concept is about skills, and these can be developed. Therefore, the results of the EQ test are about the development of skills. Where does someone stand now, and where do they want to be? There is also a 360-degree feedback version that allows the client to ask others to fill out the list, making it possible to compare their own view on emotional skills with how other people see them.

The EQ questionnaire consists of 133 questions, and the test takes about twenty minutes to complete. The test examines five dimensions, each specified by three factors. The test also indicates the general well-being of the test taker.
The test includes three control measures. Two of them indicate whether the test taker is positive or negative about their emotional skills on average. The third is an inconsistency index that provides information on the degree of consistency of the answers. This is done by asking a question in slightly different ways at different times. If an inconsistency is found based on the answers, this does not necessarily mean the questions have been answered incorrectly. However, it is a reason to check with the client why they have not responded consistently.

The first test is the baseline measurement. This test provides a profile and shows which skills the client could work on. The second time I administer the test usually isn't until six months or a year later, depending on the duration of the coaching process. This enables us to see how much progress the client has made. The EQ profile is not about getting the highest possible score. The aim is to achieve balance within the profile.

Dimensions and factors

According to the MHS EQ-i 2.0 model, emotional intelligence consists of five dimensions with three factors each:

Dimension	Factors
Self-perception	Self-regard Self-actualization Emotional self-awareness
Self-expression	Emotional expression Assertiveness Independence
Interpersonal	Interpersonal relationships Empathy Social responsibility
Decision-making	Problem solving Reality testing Impulse control
Stress management	Flexibility Stress tolerance Optimism

In practice

Just knowing about these different aspects of emotional intelligence is helpful to many clients. They can pay attention to these aspects and improve their skills. There are numerous exercises to improve emotional skills. They often start with increasing emotional self-awareness. It can be helpful to keep an emotion diary. Sometimes, working with these skills results in intense feelings of anxiety, depression, and/or shame. When this goes beyond my expertise, I have to refer clients to another mental health professional. The EQ test can give clients valuable information to bring to another mental health professional.

Many gifted people have a great sense of empathy regarding interpersonal skills. Many of my clients have difficulty setting their boundaries effectively because they strongly desire to connect with others. They have difficulty being true to themselves because of their high degree of empathy. Working on boundaries to improve emotional skills is an important theme for my clients.

4.3. Communication skills

Many requests for support in my practice concern communication skills. Much goes wrong in aligning with non-gifted people because gifted people have a different frame of reference. Their more nuanced perception, thinking more steps ahead, greater awareness, and ability to cope with greater complexity provide a different perspective. When a gifted person does not realize that not everyone has these qualities, it affects how they deal with people. When someone discovers their giftedness, this changes. My clients grow in the way they approach others and, for example, start giving information in smaller doses. They realize that someone else doesn't need thirty-four arguments in favor and seventeen against to come to a decision; as few as three arguments may be enough for that person.

Perception

Another characteristic theme of gifted people is that they can come across as somewhat threatening. This is often related to their top-down thinking, which often generates general questions in gifted people when they want to know something specific. Usually, these are questions about an underlying reason: Why was the decision made to do it this way? Who was involved in this? Why haven't we encountered this before? What purpose does this serve?
This can come across as intimidating. The other person doesn't understand why the gifted person asks these questions. Colleagues

don't understand this either. It can lead to an uncomfortable situation in which the manager or a colleague feels ridiculed, which is rarely the intention, but a consequence of perception. When they become aware of their qualities, gifted people change their "old" way of asking questions to a more pleasant way for others—no more Spanish Inquisition.

Top-down thinking can cause another communication problem. Gifted people feel the need to understand the reason why before making a choice or a decision. They may project this need when communicating with others. Therefore, a gifted person will first tell the whole story of how they got to a particular point before getting to the question, the choice, or the announcement. Another person may interpret this as a form of justification or uncertainty. Sometimes the other person "loses interest" because they (the non-gifted person) do not appreciate a lengthy explanation beforehand. Therefore, I advise my clients to start with the point they want to make. If the person they're talking to has questions, they will ask, and the gifted person can then provide a further explanation. This approach is much more effective because the gifted person will also know when the other person has a question and will thus listen to the explanation.

Communication aspects

The simplest communication model I have ever found (source unknown) says that communication has three characteristics: content, process, and relationship. In good communication, content is supported by a basis of process and relationship. When content is emphasized, the triangle becomes unstable. One small push will cause the triangle to collapse.

The following diagram represents this:

Three aspects of communication

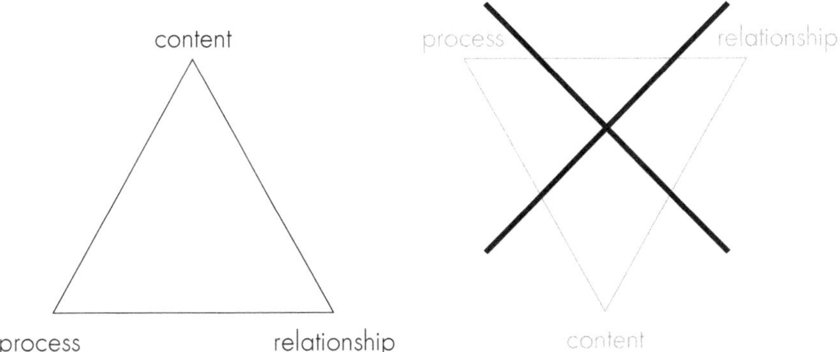

Gifted people prefer to start with the content because that is where their strength lies. Unfortunately, they forget about the process and the relationship, which are often less important to them. A client once told me: "I don't have to like a colleague to be able to work well with them." While that may be true, colleagues can achieve a lot more much quicker if they have a good relationship.

The process aspect of communication can be observed from a bird's-eye view. How does communication proceed? Do the participants listen to the speaker? Do people let each other have their say? Does everyone get a chance to speak? Many of my clients aren't concerned with this aspect of communication in everyday life, but they quickly learn once it is pointed out to them. Becoming aware of it is usually enough to realize that "process-based" interventions in communication are effective.

The relationship aspect of communication includes questions like: Do we like each other? Are there emotions at play below the surface? What is the balance of power like? Is there a feeling of "us"? That should also be appreciated and receive enough attention. Many gifted people feel strong resistance here. Attention must be paid to the relationship to ensure that content is received properly and to get someone on board. Being right is about the content, but being acknowledged is about the relationship and the process. Some of my clients can do this already, while others find it awful and, perhaps for that reason, even get angry about it: "If the content is correct, it should be fine. That's what it's all about." These clients usually need to develop the "process" and "relationship" aspects further.

Opening and closing

It is easier to avoid this typical pitfall in written communication. In that case, the order is unimportant, so a gifted person can follow their order. For example, when receiving a question by email, a gifted person can immediately respond in terms of content.
They can then add the opening and closure to their content-based response. They can use an introductory sentence to express appreciation or interest in someone or thank them for something. And there is a closing sentence at the end of the message. For example: "I hope I have answered your question correctly, but please let me know if you have any more questions."

This is more difficult in spoken communication. You cannot start with the content if you also want to consider the relational aspect. It is not possible to apply changes afterward unnoticed. The order of spoken communication is therefore essential. An interpersonal connection must be made first, followed by the content. The road has to be paved before anything can travel over it. Unfortunately, gifted people often forget the latter because their love of efficiency is too great; it's much faster to get right to the point, isn't it?

4.4. Effective influencing

Gifted people often feel misunderstood and become frustrated when others do not see where they are headed. It is thus important that gifted people provide information in small doses when explaining their views to others. Large volumes of information can cause others to feel overwhelmed, lose track, or lose interest.

These responses are ineffective. In these instances, information should be provided in small doses. Repetition can also be useful. But that is difficult, especially for someone who needs little to no repetition themselves. A pitfall, causing reproaches to lurk: "I already said that three weeks ago." This sounds like the other person is being blamed, while the expectation that the other person still remembers is a projection of the gifted person's ability. Non-gifted people remember a specific situation and not the rule behind it, representing bottom-up versus top-down. As a result, a theme or a story may be mentioned repeatedly. When a gifted person does not realize that this is how it works, it can become problematic.

I often tell my clients about the seed metaphor for effectively influencing others. For a gifted person, harvesting happens fairly soon after sowing. Still, for non-gifted people who cannot to cope with the same complexity or high pace as a gifted person, it is vital to water the seed and fertilize it after a few days, after which the seed will germinate. Gifted people must let go of the assumption that everyone knows, understands, and can reproduce after hearing something just once.

For introverted gifted people, this again works differently. They rarely say too much, but they must also learn to dose information. With more introverted gifted people, I often work on how they can communicate *more.*
Projecting themselves or being visible is another theme their environment often suggests as an "area of improvement." Speaking out more often and involving others in the process are often the skills to be developed. I think it is essential that this happens authentically. There is a difference between aligning and adapting. Adapting is not authentic and usually means that someone goes against their principles. To me, aligning means choosing deliberately from a personal palette of options. My esteemed colleague Frans Corten also uses these words in his book *Exceptional Talent.* I recommend this book to many of my clients.

4.5. Executive functions

Executive functions are skills that help you manage yourself.
You use them to organize activities, and they are underlying
and helpful. An example of an executive function is planning. In
the world of gifted children, the need for planning is virtually
nonexistent because their high intelligence and sizeable working
memory make this unnecessary, compensating for the use of this
executive function. The same applies to other executive functions.
Appropriate and sufficiently challenging education is needed to
ensure that gifted children learn these skills.
Underdevelopment of these skills can lead to problems later in
life. In adulthood, challenges and responsibilities are generally
more substantial, complex, serious, unpredictable, and changeable
than in childhood. If executive functions are not adequately
developed during childhood, this significantly impacts the adult's
self-management.

Peg Dawson and Richard Guare are psychologists who specialize
in executive functions. According to them, these skills are mostly
biologically defined. Together with Chuck Martin, they wrote
the book *Work Your Strengths: A Scientific Process to Identify Your
Skills and Match Them to the Best Career for You*, published in 1994.[3]
They write that people can no longer learn executive functions
from the age of twenty-six because that is when the brain stops
developing. Thus, in their opinion, you should match your job
to the executive skills mastered by that age. When I read that, I
was surprised, to say the least. I couldn't believe it was true, and
I wrote a blog about it in 2016. That same year, Peg Dawson and
Richard Guare published *The Smart but Scattered Guide to Success:
How to Use Your Brain's Executive Skills to Keep Up, Stay Calm, and
Get Organized at Work and at Home*, a special edition for adults.[4]
In this book, they revisit the inability to learn new skills after
twenty-six. New insights in neurology indicate that the brain

---

3 Dawson, Guare, 1994
4 Dawson, Guare, 2016

can create new neural pathways in later life by neuroplasticity. This process takes longer than in children or younger people, but adults can also strengthen their executive functions with enough practice and perseverance. Thank goodness.

Measuring executive functions

The 2016 book for adults includes a questionnaire that people can use to measure their executive functions. It can be downloaded free of charge from the publisher's website. I regularly use this questionnaire in my practice. A client fills in the questionnaire, and I let them ask people in their environment to fill out the questionnaire with the client in mind. A client's colleagues or family members may view their skills rather differently than the client themselves. These differences provide topics of conversation and are often very informative.

The questionnaire covers the following twelve executive skills:
1. Response inhibition: The ability to think first and then act. This ability to resist the urge to say or do something gives us time to evaluate a situation and how our possible response may impact it.
2. Working memory: The ability to memorize information while performing complex tasks. This ability involves applying previously learned skills or experiences to the current or future situation.
3. Emotional control: The ability to manage emotions to achieve goals, complete tasks, or control and direct behavior.
4. Task initiation: The ability to start projects on time, efficiently, and without procrastinating.
5. Sustained attention: The ability to stay focused on a situation or task despite distraction, fatigue, or boredom.
6. Planning/prioritization: The ability to make a plan to achieve a goal or complete a task. This executive function also relates to the ability to decide what is important and what is not.

7. Organization: The ability to create and maintain systems to keep track of information or materials.
8. Time management: The ability to estimate how much time you have, how best to allocate it, and how to meet a deadline, realizing that time is important.
9. Flexibility: The ability to revise plans when faced with obstacles or setbacks, new information, or mistakes. This concerns adapting to changing conditions.
10. Metacognition: The ability to take a bird's-eye view of yourself in a situation. It is the ability to observe how you solve problems. It is also about self-monitoring and self-evaluation, for example, by asking yourself: "How am I doing?" Or: "How did I do?"
11. Goal-directed persistence: The ability to formulate a goal, achieve it, and not be distracted or deterred by competing interests.
12. Stress tolerance: The ability to thrive in stressful situations and cope with uncertainty, change, and performance demands.

Everyone has more and less strongly developed executive functions. The questionnaire includes a few questions about each executive function. The answers result in a profile. I have quite a few clients with many poorly developed executive skills. The results of the questionnaire work at different levels and indicate which executive functions are strongly, less strongly, or poorly developed.

Together with the client, I will look at how they can adequately manage their weaker executive functions. To do so, we consider the client as well as their environment:

- Can the stronger executive functions be used to compensate for the weaker ones?
- Can the weaker executive functions be further developed?
- How can we use the people in the client's environment so that they are less affected by their weaker executive functions (and benefit more from their strong executive functions)?

It benefits the client to know their weaknesses. This helps because one person cannot do everything.

Many of my clients find the profile based on this questionnaire from Dawson and Guare's book enriching.

Dealing with weaker executive functions

I am more focused on talent than on competency. In talent development, the approach is that clients work mainly on their strong talents because that is where they can excel and derive pleasure from. Competency management is working on what should be improved. And thus, the focus is on what does not go well. While people can benefit from improving weaker skills, there is also a downside to focusing on what isn't going well. When a client experiences difficulties due to a poorly or undeveloped executive skill, we look at how they can work on it and make a plan. This can be done in various ways, with their environment also playing a role: sometimes it is possible to make changes in the environment so that the client is not as affected by a weaker executive skill. For example, if a client is poor at a particular executive skill while a colleague is very good at it, they can agree to do things for each other. They will both be engaged in activities that energize them, and the work gets done faster. Or, if a gifted employee is not very good at time management, but a colleague is, they can make arrangements with each other. In that case, the colleague could regularly check in with the gifted person so that they can then reflect together. This makes it easier for the gifted employee to meet project deadlines. Many of my clients have difficulty asking for help, so I also address this during my coaching.

When a client wants to improve a weaker executive function, it is best to use their stronger executive functions. Someone will never become good at an executive function for which they have no aptitude, but strengthening that skill can make it less of a problem.

Dawson and Guare's book also offers advice on how to develop skills, and I often use it to create an action plan with the client. I also use the CoreTalents Analysis for this. It may be that someone has not yet developed the skills corresponding to a strong CoreTalent. Working on this is positive because it energizes the client and results in a steep learning curve. But when a weakly developed executive function aligns with a CoreTalent that is a small talent in the client's constellation, it doesn't make much sense to invest in this skill. In that case, it simply isn't in the client's nature and does not provide much energy. At best, you can raise the skill to an acceptable level to reduce the burden on the client. But in these situations, I focus more on exploring what can be changed in the environment or how other skills can compensate.

4.6. Study skills

Many of my clients never completed their studies. Once they discover their giftedness, they often understand why. Many of them want to go back to school and earn a degree. They want to find a job that better matches their potential. Study skills are much easier to learn once the client is aware of their giftedness.

To improve study skills, I use a before-during-after outline, which is all about self-management.
How do you study? How do you work through large quantities of study materials? Suppose you go to university and you have to learn the contents of four extensive books. How do you do that? What strategy do you use? Those books can be intimidating. Most of my clients got through high school by skimming through the study book the night before a test or exam. But you cannot get away with this at university.

Study tips for gifted students:

Before	During	After
Physical: Organize your study space, minimize distractions *Content-related:* Know what you are going to do Prepare by asking questions like: What do I already know about this? What do I hope to learn now? What is the purpose of my upcoming study session? A, B, or C? Purpose of preparation: activating the system already in your mind to easily put the study materials into your system during the session	Execute according to plan/goal as determined during preparation: • A: skim through to "unlock" the book (or relevant chapter), look at its table of contents, discover its structure and layout • B: read the content of the material, take notes or make a summary (possibly in the form of a mind map) or underline definitions, important tables/illustrations • C: repeat the definitions and important tables/ illustrations 1 study session (this middle part) is no longer than 20-30 minutes at a time	Evaluate, process, reflect • What have I learned now? • What insights have I gained? • What was really new to me? • What did I already know? • Does it resemble something else I already knew? • What questions do I have for the next study session (= transition to preparing the next session)?

Some gifted people need to plan better or should focus on other executive functions. They can make studying more enjoyable for themselves by finding and using additional literature that feeds their curiosity.

Writing papers or other creative assignments

The study skills above are about learning theoretical study materials. Another study skill involves creation. For example, if my clients have to write a paper, I use the creation styles of Mozart and Beethoven.

Planning

Planning is a necessity for memorizing large amounts of knowledge or writing assignments. If someone has to study the contents of four extensive books, how long should the study sessions be? How do they schedule their study sessions? What deadlines do they use? Thus, executive functions also play an essential role in studying.

Using

By this phase in the coaching process, the client knows a lot about giftedness and its implications. The client can deal with it and has adapted their behavior to this knowledge. They have also practiced new behavior. Now it is time to look at the client's environment. What does the client want to do with their life? Career and finding meaning are major themes in this phase.

5.1. Using CoreTalents

The CoreTalents Analysis provides a compass for the rest of the client's life. The client should recalibrate it regularly. Are they using their strong CoreTalents? Which are and which aren't, or not enough? The client can then make adjustments accordingly.

Gifted clients are a highly diverse population, but there are always some common themes: they have high levels of autonomy, creativity, and strategic insight. However, this does not apply to every gifted individual.
Non-gifted people have an average of nine or ten strong CoreTalents. My clients have an average of fifteen, but some have more than twenty.
Having so many CoreTalents makes it challenging to look for and find one specific passion. This is why gifted people are often unable to find help in regular career coaching. This coaching is based on the assumption that everyone has one passion.
Emilie Wapnick gave a TED Talk that is popular among gifted people – *Why some of us don't have one true calling* – in which she introduced the term 'multipotentialities.' I often show my clients her lecture, with which many of them identify.

Our society inhibits the great intrinsic motivation of people with many strong CoreTalents. Performing the CoreTalents Analysis gives my clients the acknowledgment and confirmation they need. Many of them do things that are not possible according to prevailing standards and are sometimes even contradictory.

For example, they enjoy working in teams as much as working alone. They don't want to and don't have to choose. In our society, it is normal to think in terms of opposites and either/or. But gifted people often think in terms of and/and. They are often both specialists and generalists. Many gifted people become specialists in several areas during their lives. Chaos and structure can also unite themselves in one person. They may be organized in one area and chaotic in others. They are often both rational and empathetic. We call these life paradoxes. The more strong CoreTalents someone has, the more paradoxes exist.

5.2. Applying for jobs

A job candidate shows their best side on their résumé. Some things are overemphasized, while others are underemphasized. This increases the candidate's chances of being invited for an interview.
The same applies to employers. The organization's website features beautiful pictures and inspiring stories about its mission and vision. And the job description provides an idealized representation of the job. Tasks, responsibilities, and authorizations do not always turn out as described in the job ad.

Many of my clients find it stressful to apply for a job. They feel like they have to sell themselves to an employer.
I also often see that my clients only apply for jobs that look perfect on paper. This places them in a subordinate position: the employer has something they want, and they are not allowed to fail during the job interview.
I do not consider this approach useful, so I advise my clients to apply for anything that *might be of interest*. This way, they go into the interview with a more inquisitive approach. Adopting the attitude, "I'm coming to find out what the reality is; it probably won't live up to the job description" gives them more room.
I also advise my clients to look at factors that are not apparent

from the job description: What are the building and the working environment like? What are the manager and the company culture like? What opportunities for development are there? These are all important factors that do not become evident until the application process.

The applicant also has something to offer: commitment, knowledge, and qualities. You don't want to sell them to just anyone!

So my message is that lower or realistic expectations can positively influence a client's job application process. Clients should remember that they might discover that the job isn't right for them during the interview and that that's okay. They explored the job opportunity, but it turned out not good enough.
I also recommend being interviewed more frequently so that clients can become better at job interviews.

The application process is a ritual of introduction for two parties exploring whether they want to move forward together. Many of my clients do not realize that being offered a job doesn't mean they have to take it.

The job application process includes multiple subjective components, such as assessing the résumé. Give your résumé to five different recruiters, and you will get five different assessments.

Themes that gifted people often encounter during the application process:

- **The gifted applicant's level of education is lower than required for positions that could be suitable.**
  Many gifted people have not had successful academic careers. Often, they have not earned degrees. How can they get a job at a level that matches their professional and intellectual ability?

- **Wanting to do something they have never done before: a new challenge.**
  Often, a gifted person who wants to take a career step is ready for something new. That means they want to do something they have never done before, which their résumé does not include. Recruiters often search the résumé for evidence that someone has held a similar position before. Therefore, a gifted person must make an extra effort to show the recruiter that this step follows logically from previous work experience.
- **Having done many different things and never having stayed anywhere for long.**
  Jack of all trades, master of none. Many gifted people quickly become bored with a job, especially if it is below their level. This can lead to many different employers and short-term employment contracts on their résumés. A potential employer may wonder whether to invest in this person, as their chances of staying for a long time are considered low.
- **There has been a previous labor dispute.**
  Particularly in relation to the previous point, I see that many gifted people leave jobs following a labor dispute. When preparing for job interviews, I work with clients on developing good stories that allow them to explain their reasons for leaving previous jobs in a neutral way.

5.3. Being self-employed

During the coaching process, many of my clients discover that they no longer want to work for a boss. Research by Reijseger, Peeters, and Taris in 2013 and 2014 shows that many gifted people feel more comfortable being self-employed. It gives them the space to work on their terms: they can be their autonomous selves. I also use the CoreTalents Analysis for this. Even if the CoreTalents related to "putting yourself in the spotlight" are small, meaning that sales and commerce are not strong talents, we can find a way to make self-employment work. A client can then use their creativity, for example, to make a good website as a sales channel.

5.4. Finding meaning

Many clients already have questions about finding meaning before starting the coaching process. For others, such questions may arise during the process. For example, a client may wonder whether being gifted also means they have to deal with global issues such as sustainability, justice, and climate change. Does this gift come with an obligation? Because gifted people can think so many steps ahead, they can imagine an ideal world. Many gifted people are genuine idealists. The drawback to this is that everyday reality can let them down and that gifted people have to learn to deal with disappointments. The perfect picture is also created based on high sensitivity and a great sense of empathy.

Many gifted people want to feel connected to something bigger than themselves. While this probably also applies to non-gifted people, I strongly see it in my gifted clients. When this connection fails to materialize, there is no sense of purpose, and there is a risk of depression. Some may be in danger of having thoughts such as "nothing matters" or "life has no meaning." Others may even have suicidal thoughts.

It is essential to pay attention to these thoughts related to finding meaning. And not just to the rational side, but also the emotional side. I use James T. Webb's book *Searching for Meaning* in these cases. In the United States, achievement and excellence are greatly emphasized. The cognitive aspects are highly valued, while there is often less attention to emotional, sensitive, and spiritual aspects. For this reason, James T. Webb established SENG (Supporting the Emotional Needs of the Gifted) forty years ago. This organization aims to recognize and acknowledge the emotional side of giftedness and support gifted people in this respect.

Idealism leads to disappointments, but the fact that you can see so many steps ahead also provides a direction and gives hope. Webb's book *Searching for Meaning* is about this hope and meaning in life. Gifted people feel the need to work on their legacy. It is about leaving something good behind. Webb's book fulfilled this role for himself. It is about how idealism in gifted people can genuinely work.

My advice to my clients is to let the number of steps you can think ahead be an inspiration and try to steer your own course.

I also often use the previously discussed "Circle of 8" in this phase of the coaching process. When they feel powerless, I try to get my clients on the track of influence. Many gifted people find meaning in "big" themes. I then ask them: "What can you contribute?"

I also think formulating a personal mission statement is an excellent assignment to support this. The assignment is based on the work of Stephen Covey, who wrote *The 7 Habits of Highly Effective People*. Chapter 2 of that book is about "beginning with the end in mind." The reader is invited to imagine attending their own funeral. Who will speak there? And what would you like these people to say about you? This can then be further elaborated in the roles people play in life and the values they pursue.

The environment

When gifted adults start exploring their recently discovered giftedness, they uncover a lot and finally recognize their giftedness. Many things fall into place, and their giftedness is finally recognized and acknowledged. It is inevitable that this also affects the people in their environment. Being confronted with the gifted person's feelings of grief and euphoria sometimes demands a lot of the people around them. In addition, the gifted person's behavior changes. Here too, some people have an easier time accepting this than others. Relationships can grow deeper, but they can also fall apart. And everything in between, of course.

The people in a gifted person's environment play a major role in why a client becomes aware of the theme of 'giftedness.' For example, because one of their children is found to be gifted, it prompts the unknowingly gifted parent to start reading more, after which they identify with many of the characteristics themselves. They realize that it is also about them.
It could also be that someone close to them suggests they are gifted. That might be a good friend, family member, or colleague. Noks Nauta, one of the founders of the IHBV (Dutch Gifted Adults Foundation), suggests that conflicts in the workplace also often lead people to discover that they are gifted.

6.1. Partner, parents, children, and friends

When adults start dealing with their newly discovered giftedness, this has consequences, especially for their family members. Often, discovering that a child in the family is gifted leads a parent to discover their own giftedness. I often hear that the gifted child is like a mirror for the gifted parent. The parent's coping process evokes many emotions and causes the parent to want to reconsider their childhood from a different perspective. This can confront them with a disproportionate emotional burden from time to time, which can sometimes result in intense and passionate discussions with teachers at their child's school, for example, as they relive their childhood. The gifted parent wants to prevent their child from going through the same difficulties they went through.

Partner

The relationship with their partner may also become strained. The situation is different when both partners discover their giftedness, but even then, their individual processes are often out of sync. This does not necessarily mean the relationship will deteriorate. On the contrary, some relationships grow deeper and stronger. Unfortunately, many relationships fall apart. Once someone discovers their giftedness, their self-image changes to such an extent that the relationship cannot survive.
In my practice, I also often see gifted women with an older partner who is not gifted. You also see this among gifted children: they often have friends who are a few years older. They experience more reciprocity in such a relationship. Life experience bridges the intelligence gap. But as they grow due to personal development, the gifted person can outgrow the non-gifted person. Not every relationship can withstand such a change.

The discovery process can put much strain on partners, especially if one partner is not gifted. For example, they may experience a sense of powerlessness regarding the gifted partner's feelings of grief. Conversely, they may suddenly see their partner bursting with the energy released and not know how to respond. Both the sadness and the euphoria are hard for them to understand and thus difficult to cope with. Partners see it happening but don't always understand what they see or how they can support their gifted partner.
And then there is the behavioral change. The gifted partner leaves behind certain behavior and sometimes acquires new behavior almost automatically. The people in the gifted person's environment have to adapt to this new behavior. Is that possible? Is the new behavior accepted? If it is not, the people in the gifted person's environment often want them to return to their old

behavior, resulting in a struggle that may lead to the end of the relationship. Sometimes, a change of environment is the only way a gifted person can change. After all, the new environment does not expect them to show their old behavior.

Parents and grandparents

Parents are another potential issue for a gifted adult. Many gifted people feel the need to discuss their giftedness with their parents. Unfortunately, not every client still has their parents. Sometimes the relationship is complex, and their need to talk does not go down well. The client's adult view on their childhood changes and leads to conclusions or findings that their parents may not necessarily share or appreciate.

Clients also sometimes see characteristics of giftedness in their parents, which makes sense given its hereditary component.
A client may have a growing need to know this and to make it explicit, but their parents do not necessarily share this need. Other family members, such as siblings and cousins, are often included in the evaluation process. Especially during the period of temporary extra focus on giftedness, the whole family is analyzed.
For older generations, giftedness has not always manifested itself in great achievements, for example, due to the position of women or the social status of people in general. As a gifted person learns more about the characteristics of giftedness, they can more easily recognize those characteristics in the older generations.

Friends

The process also has consequences within circles of friends. Certain friends may also turn out to be gifted. Other friends are left behind, especially if the relationship was already rocky beforehand. It becomes evident that the desired reciprocity doesn't exist.

I also often see clients seeking contact with classmates from elementary school and high school. This triggers memories about teachers, and they identify those who were probably gifted.

Clients will rethink all of their relationships. The effect of the discovery always extends beyond the gifted person themselves.

Contact with other gifted people

One of the things I recommend to my clients is to seek out other gifted people actively. The Mensa society facilitates this peer contact but is only open to people with an IQ score in the top two percentiles. Organizations like the Dutch Gifted Adults Foundation (*Instituut Hoogbegaafdheid Volwassenen*, IHBV) and the Gifted! Foundation (*Stichting Hoogbegaafd!*) do not have an IQ requirement and also organize many gatherings for gifted people. Peer contact lets gifted people encourage one another. Receiving confirmation further reinforces their identity.

Clients often feel a deep connection with other gifted adults, which can lead to confusion relating to intimacy, love, and/or sex. A client may feel a never-before-experienced connection to another gifted person, which can be very confusing, especially during the discovery period. And not just for the client themselves, but also for the people in their environment.

It may be that the connection someone feels to another gifted person goes deeper than their connection to their partner, even if it remains platonic. That is scary but can also be liberating for the client. However, the partner, who is not part of this new relationship, may feel threatened. It is hard for the partner to see that their other half has an intimate connection with someone else and cannot have the same connection themselves. This can lead to feelings of jealousy and/or not being good enough.

This is complicated. I regularly organize workshops for partners of gifted people in which they can share these experiences. I notice that they also need this peer contact.

Support from the environment

When a gifted person starts talking about their process with others, the people in their environment can support them. A gifted person who "comes out" has to indicate their needs. They have a new outlook on life because of this theme. They can only do this in their own time and at their own pace. The people around them need to realize how intense this process can be for the gifted person.

There are also cases in which a gifted person does not share their discovery. Perhaps the fear of rejection is too great. They then painstakingly hide their discovery until they are certain. These clients often want to take an intelligence test to prove their story to others.

The support provided by people in their environment often consists of listening and giving them space to go through the discovery process. In the context of work, employers can also help figure out how to make jobs suitable and keep them challenging. An employer can also be supportive by providing allowances for training courses or coaching programs.

6.2. Colleagues and managers

After discovering their giftedness, many of my clients start to see and judge things differently at work, such as how they relate to colleagues and managers. They often become better at expressing their needs and boundaries. A situation at work can also prompt the discovery process.

Some of my clients are on long-term sick leave. Their getting sick is almost always related to their giftedness or high sensitivity. Fortunately, more and more occupational physicians are aware that giftedness is a possible explanation. The possibility is often raised when difficulties working with others or a conflict in the workplace occur.

My clients often wonder whether or not to bring up their giftedness at work or during a job interview. I see that their desire to do so is related to the phase in their process.
During the early stages of the discovery phase, there is often a strong urge to tell everyone. This sometimes leads to unpleasant reactions because the people in the gifted person's environment don't always respond positively and have many preconceptions. Lack of knowledge plays a major role. People may also say: "Yes, of course, I've known that for a long time."

I see that clients who did not complete their education at their cognitive level have a strong desire to find another job after discovering they are gifted. They want to find something more suited to their cognitive level. Some clients also want to go back to school if the process releases their developmental potential. Or their manager notices the change, and the client responds that they want a more challenging job. They then look at opportunities for development within the organization. Of course, the options also depend on the work context and what is possible there, and clearly, the process has consequences. An adaptive environment ensures that great strides can be made during this process. Contexts that do not or cannot adapt lead to sick leave or dismissal. Sometimes a client will courageously decide that things are not going to work out and starts looking for something else. This sometimes ends in a settlement agreement with outplacement in which various aspects, such as education, can be negotiated.

As with their friends, many gifted people also recognize other gifted people among their colleagues. This is also how giftedness crossed my path. Employers can certainly be supportive in this process. Organizations with knowledge about giftedness are often supportive already. These organizations respond to the potential of the gifted people who work for them and organize (management) development programs. Performing markedly better than other employees provides opportunities for both the employee and the employer.

During or after the discovery process, many gifted people consult with their managers, HR, the occupational physician, or another trusted person, making those in their environment more aware of their giftedness. The organization will then look into whether it has any other gifted employees. I can attest to that because more and more employers invite me to give presentations. The aim is often to increase awareness among employees who are not yet aware of their giftedness. The employer then plays a supporting role. The Ambassador for Giftedness (*Ambassadeur Hoogbegaafdheid*) training program I developed with a project team through my company *Hoogbegaafd in Bedrijf* (Gifted in Company) is an excellent way for gifted employees to put the theme on the map at work.

In 2012, Nauta, Ronner, and Brasseur surveyed Mensa members, asking what they considered to be the ideal manager. The results were all rather obvious. Gifted people want to be treated with sincerity, equality, and integrity, just like everyone else, but gifted people react more strongly when this does not happen. Their strong sense of justice and strong principles have a high impact when rules are disregarded. This is also related to their high sensitivity and nuanced perception. Gifted people are also more likely to see inconsistencies, resulting in discovering structural errors much earlier. What others see as unrelated incidents may signify a structural problem to a gifted person. I often recognize characteristics of giftedness in stories of whistleblowers.

6.3. Mental health professionals

People usually come to my practice once they are already consciously working on the theme of 'giftedness.' But what if you, as a mental health practitioner, suspect your client may be gifted, and your client is still unaware of this? My advice is to tell them, but allow the client their own process. Sometimes it is not the first time someone has been told they might be gifted, but they haven't been ready to deal with it yet. You can help your client by referring them to the general literature about giftedness available in your country.

The advice to give the client room to take on the theme of 'giftedness' is based on autonomy. A gifted client decides for themselves when to start working with the theme. If you do not respect this autonomy, you risk pushing the client away. Getting started with it is a great catalyst and makes people stronger. Sometimes this will be the first time a person hears they might be gifted and quickly dismiss it. But it is also possible that this is not the first time and that being told this again prompts them to really get involved with the theme.

There are several good books on giftedness for psychologists, psychotherapists, and psychiatrists. Previously, I mentioned the book *Misdiagnosis and Dual Diagnoses of Gifted Children and Adults* by James T. Webb. I consider this book to be mandatory reading for mental health professionals.

Many gifted people have run into problems earlier in their lives and ended up in the regular mental health care system. This is not a positive experience for everyone, especially if their giftedness is not recognized.

Sometimes things go well, but unfortunately, there are more cases where things did not turn out well. If a gifted person does not feel at ease and the mental health professional only considers the disorders in the DSM, this often results in misdiagnosis. Many of the behaviors of gifted people can be interpreted as symptoms of DSM diagnoses. This is not helpful to gifted people. In addition, gifted people are good at concealing things, resulting in diagnoses that are sometimes missed.

Fortunately, refresher courses for mental health professionals are slowly but surely including more knowledge about giftedness. However, this is not yet the case in their initial training. There is still much work to be done here.

Conditions for therapy

During a 2017 masterclass at the Dutch mental health education institute RINO Zuid, American psychotherapist Lisa Erickson and the participants drew up a list of conditional factors for treating gifted clients.

There are fourteen factors to be considered during therapy:
1. Ensure equality in the relationship between the client and the therapist.
2. Do not provide preliminary, quick recommendations.
3. Consider the client's strengths and abilities use them to build the relationship.
4. Do not engage in an intellectual showdown.
5. Take time to allow trust and safety to grow in the therapeutic relationship.
6. Pay attention to what is going on now, not just to what has been or is yet to come.
7. Allow attention and time for the process. Use the brakes from time to time.
8. Realize that evidence-based practices do not work. (Often, these have not been studied among gifted people).
9. Understand the gifted person's sense of humor.
10. Be transparent about the therapeutic process. (Why do you do what you do?)
11. Pay attention to the process and to the results (the process is easily neglected due to quick thinking).
12. Allow room to learn (make mistakes).
13. Make sure you have explicit knowledge about giftedness.
14. Really understand what giftedness is.

In cooperation with the IHBV, Manon Savelkoul conducted an exploratory study into the experiences of gifted people within a therapeutic relationship. She interviewed 17 gifted adults who were in therapy with a licensed psychotherapist. Unfortunately, this study has not yet been published.

The following factors in the therapeutic relationship were identified as effective:

1. The therapist is transparent in their opinions, thoughts, and actions.
2. The therapist involves the client's knowledge, understanding, and insight in the therapy.
3. The therapist takes the client's criticism seriously in a relaxed manner.
4. The therapist approaches the client's personal traits positively.

Gifted people seek contact at various levels in their relationships with mental health professionals. This may feel uncomfortable for some mental health professionals. The attitude adopted by mental health professionals in their contact with gifted clients greatly impacts the success of their treatment.

Maintaining

During the final sessions, the client and I reflect on the process together. Have the agreed goals been achieved? Which ones have, and how? Which ones have not, and why? It is essential that clients maintain their development process and can continue without my guidance.

7.1. My working method during the coaching program

At the beginning of the coaching program, I offer a free intake interview. I ask the client to fill out an intake form beforehand. One of the questions on this form is about the goals of my coaching. What does the client want to change? What does the client want to achieve? During the intake interview, I explain my working method, and we look at whether and how I can support the client in their goals. I also ask each client what they want to see changed before parting ways again.
We discuss the same points during the final evaluation. Of course, the client or I can also make adjustments along the way. Actually, I evaluate during every session. I ask my clients to write a reflection on each session. It is for the clients themselves. They may share it with me, but they don't have to. What is nice about the reflections is that they show the client's new insights and the intentions these lead to, which the client can then start working on.

I write a summary of each session, which I share with the client. Many of my colleagues find this very labor-intensive, which it is, but it is also my personal way of wrapping up. Writing a session report helps me clear my head. This became a necessity as the number of clients grew a few years ago. With thirty to forty different clients, things can easily get mixed up. My associative brain creates all sorts of connections. My reports ensure that I conclude each session in my head and that, for the next session, I exactly know what happened during the previous session with this client.

It also has advantages for the clients themselves. Many of my clients like to receive these session reports.
As well as this session report, I will also send them the illustrations used during the session.
At least some of my clients keep a personal record of the coaching process, which they can revisit if they want to. They also often draw things in their journals. The creativity of my clients produces unexpected and beautiful results.
This also shapes the journey that each client embarks on with themselves.

In my view and experience, gifted people must look at themselves from the concept of giftedness. My clients need to see how it works, and it is useful to go through this process and meet people with similar experiences. This helps my clients develop a more realistic self-image. Living with the word 'gifted' helps. Clients can use the word 'gifted' as a reference, look up its meaning, obtain information, and share experiences, opening up perspectives and leading to changes in behavior.

After completing the coaching process, a client should be able to carry on without me. I work toward that during our final sessions. I am happy to guide my clients for a while but also happy when I'm no longer needed. I try to get to a point where the client can continue the personal development process themselves. To explain this further, I touch on Dabrowski's theory and the term 'autotherapy' in the next section.

7.2. Theory of positive disintegration (Dabrowski)

Many gifted people identify with Dabrowski's theory of positive disintegration, which is a personal development theory. A long time ago, I took a course about Dabrowski with two specialists in the Netherlands. I had signed up for the part about adults and spent several days learning about Dabrowski's theory. You can find my summary in the References.

Dabrowski's theory of positive disintegration provides hope because suffering as it occurs during a personal crisis, burnout, breakdown, or depression is helpful. This suffering is needed for big growth spurts. While suffering, old mechanisms break down and create room for new ones. When someone endures a crisis well, they take a big step in their personality development.

A small part of Dabrowski's complex theories is about overexcitabilities, often taken out of context as a separate theory. According to Dabrowski, overexcitabilities are areas of sensitivity that help determine people's developmental potential. They are areas of sensitivity at psychomotor, sensual, intellectual, imaginational, and emotional levels.

Dabrowski's theory is of great added value for many of my clients. Although the theory is not firmly supported scientifically, gifted people identify strongly with it.

They can take something positive from it. That dark, unpleasant, deeply emotional period in someone's life serves a purpose. It signifies growth potential, breaking old patterns to make room for new ones. Suffering is useful. That gives hope.

Like Maslow did with his "hierarchy of needs," Dabrowski described a "hierarchy" for growth potential. You can only reach the higher stage through the underlying stages.

Autotherapy

In his theory, Dabrowski also talks about autotherapy: becoming your own therapist. During the personal development process, themes or crises constantly cross your path, and you can learn to deal with them. I deliberately use this when concluding the coaching process. I recommend that both my clients and mental health professionals read more about Dabrowski's work, and especially about autotherapy.

7.3. Wrapping up the coaching process

The last session ends with questions like: What have you learned during this process? Are there valuable insights and assignments from the coaching process that you can use to tackle future themes yourself?
Clients often find keeping a journal very useful and can simply do so independently. This involves keeping a journal on a specific theme and recognizing patterns in their behavior. Clients can unleash their analytical power on themselves and use the experience gained in the coaching process.
Perhaps also other tools worked well? Which of the tools are helpful in everyday practice? Which ones does the client already use regularly? I advise each client to write down the useful tools for themselves to fall back on later.

The final questions complete the circle. Does the evaluation result in any new goals? What tools can the client use? Some clients return after a few months or years for one or more maintenance sessions. That is fine, of course. They are very welcome. However, my ultimate goal is for all of my clients to learn to manage themselves better.

7.4. Beyond the label

The client should integrate their giftedness into their "being," and they must "live" the word to move forward. But giftedness isn't everything. It is a part of someone's personality, and the weight of giftedness usually diminishes as the process progresses. I also want my clients to live a life beyond the label. The identity of my clients comprises much more than their giftedness. The label helps with personal growth, self-development, and a more positive self-image so that clients feel less like things simply happen to them and can take more control of their lives. It is both liberating and strengthening. Their existing potential is recognized and developed. Therefore, in my coaching sessions, we temporarily overemphasize the 'giftedness' aspect before integrating it into the client's self-image. The label is a means to an end, not an end in itself. It is a means to grow in personal leadership.

References

- Aron, E.N., & Aron, A. (1997). Sensory-Processing Sensitivity and Its Relation to Introversion and Emotionality. American Psychological Association, Inc.
- Barendrecht, J.(2015) Top-down denken [Top-down thinking] Chapter 25 of the book Slim 2.0 [Smart 2.0]. Published by Stichting Koepel Hoogbegaafdheid.
- Corten, F. (2021). Exceptional Talent. A Guide for the Gifted, the Inventors, and Other Birds of a Rare Feather. Published independently.
- Covey, S. (1989). The 7 Habits of Highly Effective People. Free Press.
- Dawson, P., & Guare, R. (2016). The Smart but Scattered Guide to Success: How to Use Your Brain's Executive Skills to Keep Up, Stay Calm, and Get Organized at Work and at Home. Guilford Publications.
- De Neef, M. (2010). Negatief zelfbeeld. Boom.
- Dweck, C.S. (2017). Mindset. Changing The Way You think to Fulfil Your Potential. Updated edition. Little, Brown Book Group.
- Jackson, P. Susan. (2005). The Integral Practice for the Gifted Model: developing the Whole Child and Adult. Accessed through: https://www.daimoninstitute.com/blogs/for-researchers/the-integral-practice-for-the-gifted-model-developing-the-whole-child-and-adult
- Kellogg, R.T. (1999). The Psychology of Writing. Oxford University Press.
- Kerr, B.A., & Multon, K.D. (2015). The Development of Gender Identity, Gender Roles, and Gender Relations in Gifted Students. Journal of Counseling & Development, 93(2), 183-191.

- Kooijman-van Thiel, M.B.G.M. (editor). (2008). Hoogbegaafd. Dat zie je zó! Over zelfbeeld en imago van hoogbegaafden. [Gifted. You Can See It! About Self-Esteem and Self-Image Among Gifted People]. OYA Productions.
- Martin, C., Dawson, P., & Guare, R. (1994). Work Your Strengths: A Scientific Process to Identify Your Skills and Match Them to the Best Career for You. Amacom American Management Association.
- Mendaglio S. (2008). Dabrowski's Theory of Positive Disintegration. Tucson, AZ: Great Potential Press.
- Nauta, N., & Van de Ven, R. (editors). (2017). Hoogbegaafde volwassenen, zet je gaven intelligent en positicf in [Gifted Adults, Use Your Gifts Intelligently and Positively]. BigBusinessPublishers.
- Nauta, N., Ronner, S., & Brasseur, D. (2012). Wat zijn goede leidinggevenden volgens hoogbegaafde werknemers? [What Makes Good Leaders According to Gifted Employees?] IHBV publication.
- Reijseger, G., Peeters, M.C.W., & Taris, T.W. (2013/2014). Werkbeleving onder hoogbegaafde werkers [Experiences at Work Among Gifted Employees]. Utrecht University. Report on Measurement 1 (2013), Measurement 2 (2014).
- Savelkoul, M. (2016). Wat ervaren hoogbegaafde volwassenen als werkzaam binnen een therapeutische relatie met een psychotherapeut? [What Do Gifted Adults Find Effective in a Therapeutic Relationship with a Psychotherapist?] Not yet published. Presented during Novilo/IHBV Conference 2018.
- Van de Ven, R. with the cooperation of Van der Kaaij, T., & De Mink, F. (2015). "Positive Disintegration Theory" by Dabrowski, Chapter 9 of the book Slim 2.0 [Smart 2.0]. Published by Stichting Koepel Hoogbegaafdheid.
- Van de Ven, R., Van Weerdenburg, M., & Van Hoof, E. (2016). Working with intensity; The relationship between giftedness and sensitivity in working adults in Flanders and the Netherlands. Unpublished manuscript. Accessed through: https://riannevdven.nl/publicaties/ working-with-intensity/

- Van Doorn, G., & Lingsma, M. (2017). De vijf kritieke succesfactoren voor coaching [The Five Critical Success Factors for Coaching]. Boom.
- Van Hoof, Prof. E. (2016). Hoogsensitief, wat je moet weten [Highly Sensitive, What You Need to Know]. Lannoo Campus.
- Webb, J.T. (2013). Searching for Meaning. Idealism, Bright Minds, Disillusionment and Hope. Great Potential Press.
- Webb, J.T., Amend E.R., Beljan, P., Webb, N.E., Kuzujanakis, M., Richard Olenchak, F., & Goerss, J. (2016). Misdiagnosis and Dual Diagnoses of Gifted Children and Adults: ADHD, Bipolar, OCD, Asperger's, Depression, and Other Disorders. Second edition. Great Potential Press.